DOES GOD CARE ABOUT YOUR BUSINESS?

*Discovering **God's Plan**
for Your **Business** or **Career***

RICHARD J. GROVE

All Scripture, unless otherwise marked, is from the New American Standard Bible® (NASB). Copyright © 1960, 1962, 1963, 1968, 1971, 1972, 1973, 1975, 1977, 1995 by The Lockman Foundation. Used by permission. www.Lockman.org.

All Scripture marked KJV are from the King James Version. Public domain.

All Scripture marked NIV are from THE HOLY BIBLE, NEW INTERNATIONAL VERSION®, NIV®
Copyright © 1973, 1978, 1984, 2011 by Biblica, Inc.®
Used by permission. All rights reserved worldwide.

Cover and interior formatting by
KUHN Design Group | kuhndesigngroup.com

Special Thanks to the Editors:
Caryn Rivadeneira
Pam Nordberg

Dedicated to my wife, Lisa.
None of this is possible without you.
I love you.

* * *

*A man meets a good woman
and each is made better.
What was once just enough for one
is now ample for two.
What was a struggle for two hands
is now easier done with four.
Mornings hold more promise.
Evenings bring more peace.
Hard work has a purpose
and great pleasure has a partner.
Tears don't sting
and smiles have a reflection.
Everything is made better
and God's face is more easily seen in all of it.
A man meets a good woman and God's
whole plan begins to make sense.
One trip through this life spent together with that
perfect someone is wonderfully enough.*

CONTENTS

Preface 7

1. You're Wrong 13
2. Bigger Barns 17
3. What Do You Want? 45
4. Fractions 59
5. Dangerous Territory 75
6. A Better Way 93
7. Whatever 97
8. Voices 107
9. Showing Up In the Vineyard 121
10. Garden Principle 127
11. What Then? 143
12. Amalia 149
13. Drinking the Rain 163
14. Going Home 181

About the Author 185

PREFACE

Robert was still one hundred and fifty miles from home, cruising through the night sky at an altitude of 6,000 feet. Alone in the cockpit of his single-engine Cessna, he had allowed his mind to drift back over the events of what had been an extraordinary day. It was a day he had been working toward for over a decade. The contract in his briefcase marked a turning point for him and his family. Eleven years ago, Robert had made a bold decision and walked away from a comfortable salary, a secure pension, and the stability of a large company to pursue his dream of starting his own business. Many people thought he was foolish. They said, "That is the kind of career move you make after you've lost a good job, not while you still have one."

Many times over the past eleven years, he had wondered if they were right. They had not been easy years. He had made huge sacrifices, and much of his retirement nest egg had been spent in the struggle to give legs to the new business. Fourteen-hour workdays and seventy-hour workweeks were not uncommon. In fact, they were the norm. When he was not working, he was driving, spending dozens of hours a week crisscrossing the southeast in pursuit of new clients.

The truth was that it was not the physical fatigue of the long weeks or the endless miles that troubled him, but the impact those things had upon his family. He could deal with his own sacrifices, but the ones his wife and children were making burdened him.

These concerns were Robert's primary motivation for getting his pilot's license. Flying rather than driving was supposed to allow him to spend more time at home. In reality, flying only made it possible for him to fit more meetings and sales calls into his workweek. The new contract would change everything. Now, finally, Robert was going to be able to make everything right with his family.

The deal he had negotiated earlier that day guaranteed their financial security. More importantly, he could now hire more personnel. Increasing his staff would soon enable him to slow down and spend more time with his wife and children. Feelings of pride, accomplishment, satisfaction, and relief poured through him. Robert hadn't felt this way in a long time.

He grinned as he thought about that contract locked in his briefcase and stowed behind his seat. Maybe he had missed out on some of the events in his children's lives over the past eleven years, but there were still a couple years left before his oldest would leave for college, and Robert was prepared to make the most of those years. They would take the vacations that had been talked about, promised, and then placed on hold. Robert laughed out loud thinking about how his sixteen-year-old daughter, Kelley, teased him about the fact that she had never been to Disney World.

"Deadbeat dad. I am the only person in my entire school whose parents have never taken them to Disney World. If I end up on a psychiatrist's couch one day, it will be your fault."

"That is the first trip we are going to take," Robert said to himself.

"Whether Kell wants to or not, she is going to ride every ride and sit in Mickey's lap so I can take a picture."

He would go trout fishing and camping with his son and spend long weekends with his wife in Charleston, Savannah, Asheville, and every other location she had talked about visiting. Robert could not wait to get home and tell everyone about the new contract. He had kept the possible deal a secret, fearful that it would end up falling through like many that had preceded it, just another disappointment. Tomorrow morning, he would give his wife and kids the good news. Just seeing him at home and at the breakfast table on a weekday would be a surprise for them.

Shoot, I may even get up early and make them my world-famous pancakes, Robert thought. *It's been years since I have had the opportunity to do that.* Robert closed his eyes and savored the thought of breakfast with his family. "Thank you, Lord."

Not only had Robert worked hard for eleven years but he had also spent eleven years in prayer. His word of thanks was not rhetorical; it was sincere. It was heartfelt. But it also carried a sliver of guilt. The task of building his business had kept him away from church. As hard as he had tried not to make Sunday a workday, six days were usually not quite enough. He missed the weekly fellowship of his friends at church. He missed the time that he used to spend reading and studying the Bible. For Robert, the Bible was neither mystical or magical. It was not holy gibberish, scrawled by ancient men with no contemporary application. Possessing an analytical mind as well as the self-confidence and intelligence to be a successful businessman, Robert placed a value on Scripture that seemed odd to some. Many of his peers viewed the Bible as a refuge for simple minds while he believed it to make good sense.

Robert believed Scripture to be a powerful, applicable guideline for life and business.

Although the opportunity to extensively incorporate biblical principles into his young business had not arrived, Robert intended those principles to be an integral part of the company's future growth. Robert had remained faithful in prayer when it came to his business, regularly asking the Lord's favor and blessing upon his efforts. He recognized God's omnipotence, seeking divine confirmation in the things he was doing and the decisions he was making. He read the successes and failures as signs.

"Thank you for this contract," he whispered, closing his eyes again. "It has been a long time coming. A lot has been sacrificed, and I have wondered at times if this is really what I am supposed to be doing. I realize that I probably have not been as faithful in my relationship with you, but you know how difficult and time-consuming it has been trying to get this business established. Now that I have this large contract, things are going to be different. I will increase my staff and then start enjoying life. Hopefully, as my business continues to grow, it will have the opportunity to make an impact for you."

The engine of the Cessna sputtered, and Robert's eyes flew open at the sound. It sputtered again. He looked at the gauges. The fuel pressure had dropped. He checked the tank; still plenty of fuel to get him home. The engine sputtered again. "This makes no sense."

He pushed the throttle. The engine revved for a moment, shuttered, coughed, and then went silent. An alarm in the cockpit buzzed, and the altimeter began to drop. Robert steadied the aircraft and tried to calm himself.

"You've been in this situation before. It was part of your flight training. Stay calm. Go through your check sequence and refire the engine."

Robert's mind and hands worked through the procedure for restarting the engine in flight. Through the windshield, he watched the propeller. It lurched but could not make a rotation. He tried again, begging the propeller to spin.

The altimeter was falling faster, and the air speed increased. Robert could hear the wind rushing past him and pulled back gently on the control yoke. He attempted to restart the engine again. Nothing. His plane was without power and falling from the sky. His mind raced back over all the training he had received during flight instruction. He set the transponder to 7700 and made the radio call.

"Mayday! Mayday! Mayday!"

As he made the emergency call, his mind raced with all the critical information. He checked glide angle, airspeed, and current location. Waiting a response, he thought, *This can be done; it has been done before.* He worked the yoke and the trim wheel to keep the aircraft steady on its descent. He could not help but think about the cruel irony. After struggling for eleven years to build a business for himself and his family, he had finally landed the contract that would make their dreams come true, and now it could all end one hundred and fifty miles from home. Glancing up from the instruments out the windshield, he saw the glistening stars against the black velvet sky. The scene struck him as peaceful, beautiful, and horrifying all at the same time. Robert prayed again, this time with his eyes wide open.

"Lord, please help me. I need you. Don't let it all end this way. Everything is finally working out. I need more time. Lord, please hear me."

Robert, I hear you, but there is no more time.
On this night your soul will be required of you.

・・・

And He told them a parable, saying, "The land of a certain rich man was very productive. And he began reasoning to himself, saying, 'What shall I do, since I have no place to store my crops?' Then he said, 'This is what I will do: I will tear down my barns and build larger ones, and there I will store all my grain and my goods. And I will say to my soul, "Soul, you have many goods laid up for many years to come; take your ease, eat, drink and be merry."' But God said to him, 'You fool! This very night your soul is required of you; and now who will own what you have prepared?'"

LUKE 12:16–20

CHAPTER 1

YOU'RE WRONG

"God doesn't care about our business."

My wife, Lisa, did not need to say a word; her eyes did all the talking. It was a combination of anger and disbelief, though not in equal proportion. Anger clearly dominated, and that was way out of character for my sweet Southern Baptist belle.

"How can you say something like that?" she asked. Her tone suggested that I needed to add "disgust" to the combination of anger and disbelief, giving it a portion equal to anger.

Lisa and I, along with her father, had started a business. It was a decision that had required significant financial risk. We literally staked our financial future on the success of the business, using our home and our retirement savings as collateral for a business loan. As the saying goes in poker, we were "all in." That can be very unsettling. There was reason for concern, so my wife did what any good believer does in unsettling situations: she prayed. Lisa made it a normal part of her prayer life to ask God to bless our business. In the beginning I joined her in the petition, but I was hesitant because I could not anchor my request to a particular verse or promise. Sure, there was the generic type of stuff.

> *Casting all your anxiety on Him,*
> *because He cares for you.*
>
> **1 PETER 5:7**

I found little satisfaction in that type of justification and wondered what Scripture had to say specifically about business. Having been an adult Sunday school teacher for twenty years, I had spent literally thousands of hours in Bible study. There was not a single book in either the Old or New Testament that we had not studied at least once. Although there seemed to be no topic that we had not covered, I could not draw to mind a Scripture that substantiated the prayer for blessing our business.

Rest assured, I wanted to recall one. I wanted desperately to believe that my personal relationship with the Lord afforded me a greater opportunity for business success. I needed all the help I could get, but I honestly could not put together a solid biblical argument.

I had no answers for some of the questions that Scripture raised. I had no answers for some of the things I witnessed in the business community around me. For example, even in our small town, I watched a Christian bookstore that was owned by a humble, godly family go out of business while an adult toy store opened a mile away. Which of those two do you suppose was praying for God to bless their business?

I had no answers, so I dove back into Scripture. And that return to Scripture, that search through its instructions, its exhortations, its admonitions, its parables, its examples, its characters, its historical events, its steadfast truths, and unparalleled wisdom led me to the conclusion that I shared with my wife: "God doesn't care about our business."

What I also discovered along the way was that I was okay with that. In fact, I am blessed by it.

When Lisa had settled down enough to at least listen for a moment, I read to her the "bigger barns" parable from the Gospel of Luke.

"So what?" No less disappointment in her eyes or her tone. "That's it? You have come to the conclusion that God does not care about our business based upon a parable about greed?"

"No," I said. "The 'bigger barns' parable is just part of the reason that I have come to that conclusion, but it is a pretty good starting place. There is more."

"I think you're wrong, and I don't want to listen anymore," Lisa said. "Believe what you want, but do me a favor and don't go around saying that to other people—especially our Sunday school class."

With that, my otherwise very loving, compassionate, understanding wife closed her ears to what I was learning and doubled up her prayers to compensate for my heresy.

If for no other reason, I had to write this book so Lisa could understand how I had arrived at the conclusion that she so emphatically disagreed with. I am compelled to record the things that she would not allow me to explain in person, with the hope that she would read them. I must write them down so if our children choose to follow us into business, they will understand what I believe to be its purpose.

I do not claim to be divinely gifted in discernment. I don't claim to possess theological depth. My exploration is based solely upon observation and personal interpretation. It is not my intention to manipulate Scripture to satisfy my suppositions. I gain nothing from that.

I investigated Scripture to satisfy my desire to understand God's perspective on business. As I tried to tell my wife, the bigger barns parable is a pretty good place to start.

CHAPTER 2

BIGGER BARNS

Luke 12:16–21 is not simply a parable regarding greed. It is a warning by Jesus to be on your guard against every form of greed. The warning was His introduction to the story.

> *Then He said to them, "Beware, and be on your guard against every form of greed."*
> **LUKE 12:15**

I want to place special emphasis on the word *every* because it dramatically broadens the scope of this parable. The problem is that we prefer not to consider every form of greed. Instead, we want to focus on specific greed, ugly greed, "get what you can, can what you get, sit on the lid, and poison the rest" greed. We reserve the word *greed* for cases of extreme behavior and incredibly selfish acts. Greed is for scrooges, Ponzi schemers, embezzlers, and all the other things that we could never imagine ourselves being.

In the bigger barns parable, Jesus teaches us differently. Greed comes in a variety of forms. It is not always ugly or malicious. It does not have to be blatant or obvious, and it is capable of wearing the disguise of an otherwise admirable virtue such as ambitiousness or thriftiness. In some cases, it may not appear to be greed at all. When you examine the request that triggered Jesus's warning, there seems to be nothing greedy about it.

> *Someone in the crowd said to Him, "Teacher, tell my brother to divide the family inheritance with me."*
> **LUKE 12:13**

Most people who read this would consider the person's request to be nothing less than fair. So, why did Jesus respond with a warning? He instructs us to be on our guard because greed in all its varying forms shares a common attitude, an errant belief, which is the misconception that our existence is defined by our possessions. Though society has gravitated toward this attitude, it is in direct conflict with biblical principles. Jesus discerned that the man's seemingly reasonable request was motivated by this errant belief.

> *Then He said to them, "Beware, and be on your guard against every form of greed; for not even when one has an abundance does his life consist of his possessions."*
> **LUKE 12:15**

When you consider the request of the slighted brother, and the manner in which Jesus responded, we can understand that the bigger barns parable is not addressing greed as we typically perceive it. Instead, Jesus used the story to illustrate how we are all at risk of placing too much emphasis on our possessions. The issue is not as much about greed as it is appraisal. It addresses the value we place upon the possessions we have, whether great or small.

That distinction is important because now the parable is applicable to all of us, not just those who we could never imagine ourselves being. It also makes the parable very applicable to business. In fact, if you carefully read it again, you will see that Jesus's illustration is the tale of a successful businessman. Within the verses of this intriguing parable is evidence that the man Jesus describes is not so different from the average businessman. In truth, he is very much like my fictitious character, Robert.

Is it possible that we have been too hasty and perhaps too harsh in our judgment of the central figure in Jesus's parable? If so, we are not alone. Even the commentary in my study Bible refers to this passage as the parable of the "rich fool." While both of those terms are used by Jesus in his description of the man, each deserves a more thorough investigation within the context of the story. We will begin with "rich."

It is important to understand the social and economic environment in Israel at that time. Unlike our modern society, there were not multiple levels of wealth. The line that separated the rich from the rest of society was not obscure. Although there was an economic layer, or class, between the wealthiest and the poorest (the poorest being the widows, the handicapped, the menial laborers, and the unemployable), it was not a middle class as we are accustomed to in America. The middle class was made up of the local tradesmen. In this group were the tanners, silversmiths, fishermen, weavers, and carpenters. The tradesmen were financially better off than the poorest class, but they were much too near the poor end of the scale to be considered a bridge between the upper and lower class. This was the segment of society that Jesus's family belonged to, and He was well aware of the financial separation between rich and poor. There was no gray area.

When Jesus described someone as being rich, He was placing them financially well beyond the general public.

During this period of history, the wealthy fell into one of three categories. The first group was the religious elite. Formally trained leaders of the Hebrew faith were among the wealthiest members of Jewish society. The second group was the merchant traders. They made their money buying and selling goods as commerce moved along the busy corridor that linked Asia to the Mediterranean. The last group made their money from agriculture. These were the landowners, large-scale farmers, growers of grain, figs, and grapes. The wealthy man in Jesus's parable was part of this third group.

> *And He told them a parable, saying, "The land of a rich man was very productive."*
>
> **LUKE 12:16**

I think we can all agree that wealth is not a sin. If it were, many of our Bible heroes were in trouble. The book of 2 Chronicles records the enormous wealth that was amassed by Solomon. Not many within the church criticize Solomon for his possessions, nor do they begrudge the wealth of the three gift-bearing wise men who paid homage to the Christ child. Throughout history, personal riches have not prevented God from using people for His kingdom's sake.

Though being rich is not a sin, however, there is no question that it is a formidable deterrent to godliness. Two of the New Testament's most well-known verses regarding wealth warn us of its danger. In his first letter to Timothy, Paul wrote:

> *But those who want to get rich fall into temptation and a snare and many foolish and harmful desires*

> which plunge men into ruin and destruction. For
> the love of money is a root of all sorts of evil, and
> some by longing for it have wandered away from the
> faith, and pierced themselves with many griefs.
>
> **1 TIMOTHY 6:9–10**

In the second well-known verse, Jesus was speaking to His disciples following a short conversation with a rich young man. Jesus's words regarding the potential danger of wealth astonished His disciples.

> And Jesus said to His disciples, "Truly I say to you, it is
> hard for a rich man to enter the kingdom of heaven."
>
> **MATTHEW 19:23**

That statement by itself is not so amazing. I think most of us can see how it would be difficult to maintain sincere godliness while so many of the temptations that could pull us away are within financial reach. What is astonishing is not that it is hard, but rather how hard.

> "And again I say to you, it is easier for a camel to go
> through the eye of a needle, than for a rich man to enter
> the kingdom of God." When the disciples heard this, they
> were very astonished and said, "Then who can be saved?"
> And looking at them Jesus said to them, "With people
> this is impossible, but with God all things are possible."
>
> **MATTHEW 19:24–26**

No doubt riches create an obstacle worthy of warnings, and these two Scriptures reveal that the danger posed comes in two distinctly different forms. Recognizing the differences allows us to better understand the message of each of these two popular passages from Scripture.

In Paul's letter to Timothy, he is warning of the danger that riches pose to those who have entered the faith. He said it causes them to "fall into the temptation" and "some by longing for it have wandered away from the faith." Paul is clearly speaking about those who are believers but have fallen away as a result of the "snares and harmful desires" that are associated with the "love of money." It is indeed the "root of all sorts of evil." Evil that can cause us to "pierce ourselves with many a pang." This verse is not suggesting that all relationship with Christ has ended or that those things that have been eternally gained are lost. It is a warning that we can set ourselves on a course of "ruin and destruction."

It is also important to note, as many of you are already aware, that money is not the root of all evil, but the *love* of money. That being the case, Paul makes it clear that "some" —not all— "by longing for it have wandered." It is possible to have money, even great amounts of it, and not be guilty of loving it. It is rare, but it is possible. Solomon is proof.

In the scriptural reference to riches in Matthew 19, Jesus is teaching His disciples about the danger of wealth from an entirely different perspective from the one Paul described in his letter to Timothy. In these verses, Jesus is not referring to believers who have wandered from the faith. This warning addresses the incredible obstacle that riches create for those who desire to come to Christ. The rich young man who approached Jesus in Matthew 19 wanted to know what he must do to obtain eternal life.

> *And someone came to Him and said, "Teacher, what good thing shall I do that I may obtain eternal life?"*
> **MATTHEW 19:16**

Through the course of their short conversation we discover that, although the man appears to be a morally decent person, his greatest love is the love of his possessions.

> *Jesus said to him, "If you wish to be complete, go and sell your possessions and give to the poor, and you will have treasure in heaven; and come, follow Me." But when the young man heard this statement, he went away grieving; for he was one who owned much property.*
>
> **MATTHEW 19:21–22**

Jesus is not setting a precedent that all who desire to obtain eternal life must sell everything they own. He is merely exposing the powerful hold that money and possessions can have upon men and women. Think for a moment about the deal that Jesus appears to offer this man: eternal life in exchange for his possessions. We know that Scripture makes it clear that we cannot buy our way into heaven. No amount of money is enough. As believers, we know that admission is available only through God's amazing grace, but this man would not have had that knowledge. If you listen to Jesus's offer through the ears of the rich young man, it must be taken literally. Jesus offered him eternal life in exchange for his possessions. Yet, having been offered what was undoubtedly the best deal of all time, the rich young man could not let go of the things he possessed.

Why? Because, according to Scripture, he was "one who owned much property." He chose his possessions over entrance into God's kingdom. In response to the young man's decision, Jesus explained to his disciples in descriptive terms how difficult it is for a rich man to come completely and honestly to Christ. Plainly told, it is impossible for man to do it, in and of himself. That ought to make clear to us the kind of power that the love of money wields. If we develop a love of money (or possessions) prior to a potentially life-changing encounter with Christ, we are powerless to commit ourselves to Him.

> *"And again I say to you, it is easier for a camel to go through the eye of a needle, than for a rich man to enter the kingdom of God."*
> **MATTHEW 19:24**

Those do not appear to be very good odds, but they are exactly the odds that Saul faced on the road to Damascus. What does Saul and the Damascus road have to do with "camel through the eye of a needle" odds?

Those who were formally trained and held positions of leadership within the Jewish religion were among the wealthiest members of society. That meant that in addition to his zealous hatred of new believers, Saul had both position and possessions. This was the ultimate camel-meets-needle confrontation. Saul, whom we know much better as the apostle Paul, could have never, of himself, entered the kingdom. The camel had a better chance with the needle.

Only through a supernatural encounter could a wealthy Saul have come to Christ, and only through a supernatural encounter, a spiritual transformation, could the rich young man have broken the powerful grip of "the love of money." Jesus would have willingly and joyfully produced that transformation in the young man if he had sincerely desired it. Sadly, the man could not let go of his many things. We read the scriptural account and consider it unthinkable. Yet we too are commonly bound with the chains of our own possessions; the greater our possessions, the stronger the chains that bind us.

> *When the disciples heard this, they were very astonished and said, "Then who can be saved?" And looking at them Jesus said to them, "With people this is impossible, but with God all things are possible."*
>
> **MATTHEW 19:25–26**

Simply put, Jesus could have passed the camel through the eye of the needle on the rich man's behalf had it been the sincere desire of his heart to exchange his love of money for a love of Christ. I would think that from these two Scripture references we are able to recognize that wealth is not of itself evil or ungodly, but that it has the potential to create enormous obstacles.

The point we must keep in mind is that when Jesus described the landowner in the bigger barns parable as "rich," it is not automatically a condemnation. We are quick to draw a negative opinion of the landowner based solely upon the word *rich*. It seems to be a double standard. In the Gospel of Luke we find another parable constructed around a certain man who is also a landowner. He was a man who owned property and livestock, a man who had hired help, a man with some expensive possessions. He was the father of the prodigal son and, according to Scripture, he was a wealthy man.

> *The younger of them said to his father, "Father, give me the share of the estate that falls to me." So he divided his wealth between them.*
>
> **LUKE 15:12**

For some reason, we do not apply the same negative regard to this wealthy landowner that we do the wealthy landowner in the bigger barns parable. In fact, it is quite the opposite. The rich man in the prodigal son parable is the hero, the man that we should emulate, the man who represents the person of Christ. I understand that we make our judgments with the benefit of knowing how each of the two stories end, but my point is that we need to reconsider the immediate negative perception we have of the landowner based upon the use of the word *rich*.

Understanding the economic culture of the time and mindful of the biblical perspective on wealth, we are now ready to break down the bigger barns parable from a business perspective. We will also be able to investigate why Jesus called this businessman a "fool." It should not be difficult to see parallels between the rich landowner and Robert, the businessman I wrote of in the preface.

> *And He told them a parable, saying, "The land of a rich man was very productive. And he began reasoning to himself, saying, 'What shall I do, since I have no place to store my crops?' Then he said, 'This is what I will do: I will tear down my barns and build larger ones, and there I will store all my grain and my goods. And I will say to my soul, "Soul, you have many goods laid up for many years to come; take your ease, eat, drink and be merry."' But God said to him, 'You fool! This very night your soul is required of you; and now who will own what you have prepared?'"*
>
> **LUKE 12:16–20**

Agricultural production was this man's livelihood. It was the source of his income. He was in the business of producing crops, and based upon the fact that he already had barns, we can deduce that his was an established, ongoing business. On the particular year that Jesus built His parable upon, the land had been very productive. The landowner was preparing to harvest a crop that exceeded those of previous years. Scripture does not record that the boon came at the expense of anyone else. There is no indication that it was the result of cheating, deceit, or any other form of evil or unfair conduct. The large harvest was simply the product of a very productive year.

Having lived for a time in America's heartland, I know that there are two major factors in the success or failure of a farmer's crop. The first factor is largely beyond the farmer's control. Good crops, productive years depend upon the weather. Farming, more so than any other livelihood, finds itself at the mercy of God. This was especially true prior to the introduction of science and technology. Irrigation, mechanical farming equipment, fertilizers, and pesticides aid modern-day farmers in their continuous battle with the elements. Such was not the case in Jesus's time. First-century farmers like the one in this parable had to place the success or failure of their crop largely in the hands of God. The second factor is in the hands of the farmer. Intelligent planning and good decision-making skills contribute mightily to the outcome. Both of these factors—God's hand and good management—would have contributed to the success of this landowner's crop. His efforts were about to pay dividends.

The parallel to my contemporary, first-chapter parable is obvious. Robert had put a great deal of effort into his business, and after eleven years it was on the verge of paying big dividends. It did not come about as the result of anything evil or sinister. Robert had conducted business fairly and worked hard. Though he had admittedly drifted in his relationship with God, he knew that it was by God's hand that all things were held in place. Robert had prayed for the success of his business, and in his mind, the large contract was God honoring his request.

Perhaps that is the difference we hope to find between Robert and the rich landowner. Do you suppose the landowner prayed for God to bless his crop? Do you think he prayed for God to bless his business? We automatically assume not, even though the only descriptions given in Scripture are the words *rich* and *fool*. It seems to be a commonly perceived notion that he was a godless man. If we conclude that his riches exclude him as a spiritual peer and he is not the type to pray for God's blessing, then we must also conclude that God willingly allows the businesses of those who do not acknowledge Him to prosper.

If it was God's desire to prevent this man from having a great harvest, He certainly had the means to do it. All sorts of tools were at His disposal: drought, flood, locusts, and disease. Or even the more dramatic: fire and brimstone, smoldering rocks from the sky.

Remember, this man was already successful. Barns were in place that had been used to store his crops from years past. This was not his first harvest; it was just a particularly productive harvest in a successful, thriving enterprise. Scripture does not indicate that the rich man did or did not ask God's blessing. We assume that he did not. Did God bless this man's business for years without ever being petitioned in prayer to do so? It is an interesting question, don't you think? What Scripture does indicate is that the landowner gave careful consideration to the circumstances. He deliberated; he reasoned.

> *And he began reasoning to himself, saying, "What shall I do, since I have no place to store my*

> *crops?" Then he said, "This is what I will do: I will tear down my barns and build larger ones, and there I will store all my grain and my goods."*
>
> **LUKE 12:17–18**

This is a great example of how decisions are made and problems are solved in small business—much different from large corporations. In today's large corporations, what occurred in *Luke 12:17–18* would have required six months, a couple dozen meetings, hundreds of pages of reports, charts, graphs, spreadsheets, business models, surveys, and ultimately the majority support of a board of directors. In government, the process would be twice as involved and four times more costly.

The landowner, however, like most small business owners, gathered information, considered his available options, and then devised a plan to resolve the problem. Decision-making is a critical element of success, an ongoing process that either grows or kills small business. Anyone who owns a business or holds a management position within a business must possess good decision-making skills if they are going to survive. This principle will be an integral part of our study in later chapters.

For now, it provides additional parallel between Robert and the landowner.

Based upon the landowner's decision to "tear down my barns," he evidently already had a successful, established enterprise. He owned multiple barns. He had either constructed or purchased buildings that were used to store the harvest in years past. This was not the first harvest, and based upon the fact that Scripture describes him as "rich," we must assume that he has been successful.

Such was also the case with Robert. He held a well-paid, secure position at a large company. He was drawing a large salary and accumulating a substantial retirement fund. Metaphorically, Robert already had standing barns, and by most people's standards he would also be considered rich.

Both of these businessmen could have continued to live comfortably at their current level of income. Neither required increase. The problem is that the current level is not the business plan of most successful business owners. Successful businessmen and women are looking to grow, to innovate, to become more efficient, more profitable. They are determined to improve market share and develop new markets. They cannot help themselves; it is what makes them who they are. But it does not make them evil. We are accustomed to referring to them as type A, but I think of them as people of action. People of action, people of enterprise are usually the people of choice when God wants to get something accomplished. The apostle Peter, the "rock" that Jesus desired to build his church upon was himself a solid type A, a man of action, a hardworking local businessman.

Robert and the landowner each saw an opportunity to grow their business; they saw a potential for increase. As a result, each had a decision to make, and their decisions held an element of risk. Taking a calculated chance is part of business management, and the willingness to seize those opportunities is often the difference between success and failure.

We must assume that Robert deliberated heavily before deciding to walk away from the security of a well-paying job with an established company. A person does not attain such a position without being able to weigh and reason. When he evaluated the options available, security at the current level did not appeal to Robert as much as the possibility of greater gain accompanied by risk. He made his decision.

In the case of the landowner, we do not need to speculate whether or not he deliberated over the options available, for Scripture specifically states that "he began reasoning to himself." That is very important to our understanding of this parable, and it creates a business exercise that I invite you to participate in.

The fact that he reasoned indicates that there were multiple options, each having both pros and cons. His decision, like the ones most businesspeople face every day, needed to weigh risk versus reward. What do I mean? As a society, we have, over the past couple of decades, come to embrace the phrase "no-brainer." Perhaps you have even used it yourself. "No-brainer" is used to describe a situation with an obvious clear-cut solution. Hence, you need not even apply your brain to the task. In this situation, the landowner was not faced with a "no-brainer." He had a situation that required reasoning. Put yourself in the place of the landowner. Review the options that were available to him, and then decide what you would have done.

First, let's review the problem. After several successful years in the farming business, the landowner has hit a bumper crop. He has had a "very productive" year, and the yield of the harvest is obviously going to exceed his storage capacity. It is time to make a decision, time to reason, time to develop and implement an action plan. What are the options?

OPTION #1

The first option is to simply maintain the current level. The barns are large enough to store the harvests of past years. Therefore, maximize the potential of the existing structures; harvest enough to fill the barns to their full capacity and leave what will not fit in the field. After all, that amount has always been enough. This plan has little risk, but the reward is commensurate.

Of course, the landowner could sell the portion of the harvest that will not fit into the barns. But at harvest time, the market is saturated with product. The revenue generated by the sale of excess may not bring enough money to cover the harvesting cost. This is especially true if the market understands the "must sell" position that the landowner will be in.

The other issue is that the people who will most likely need the grain over the course of the winter do not have the available capital to stockpile for future consumption. Like most of us consumers, they must buy on an "as needed" basis. I know that at our house, we do not have the ability to buy several months' worth of groceries at one time. When the kids were younger and living at home, it was a treat if groceries lasted until the end of the week.

This option also fails to address the future. I do not know of a single successful businessman who holds the belief that he cannot match or beat a previous high. The landowner had to have been certain of the possibility to have another productive harvest in future years. If nothing was done, he would face the same problem with every productive year.

OPTION #2

The second option is to add to the current capacity by leaving the current barns standing and building some more. It is the safest option for increasing capacity because it does not jeopardize the existing capacity.

Anyone who has ever been involved in a construction or expansion project understands all the things that can go wrong. Remember, the crop is already far enough along for the landowner to determine it is going to be an exceptional harvest. The harvest has either already being gleaned or it soon will be. Timing is therefore a critical issue.

Keeping his old barns standing is a good back-up plan. He will be able to maintain the previously established yield should problems arise during construction.

Leaving the existing barns standing and constructing additional new ones rather than tearing them down and starting over is also a less expensive option, with a shorter completion time. He would not need to build as much space or incur the cost of demolition. Building more barns yields a greater reward than the first option, and it does not place the crop at risk. It is a good short-term fix. The problem with this option is that it does not factor well into the long term. Adding more barns would result in less efficient land use and increased operating expenses due to multiple facilities. In addition, there would be greater maintenance costs on the aging barns.

OPTION #3

The third option is to tear down the existing barns and build larger ones. Like the second option, the bigger barns plan increases storage capacity. That addresses the immediate need, but the ideal solution also needs to satisfy the landowner's future requirements. Tearing down the existing barns and building new, larger ones accomplishes both of those objectives. The bigger barns option is an opportunity to upgrade the current facilities.

Economically, it comes at an ideal time. The exceptionally large harvest provides a window of financial opportunity. It is a plan that optimizes land use. Property that would have been used for building additional barns can be used for more productive purposes. New facilities do not require as much upkeep as older buildings. Lower maintenance costs and a more modern, efficient operation will ensure profitability well into the future. It could also prove to be a strong business move. The landowner would be recognized as a dynamic leader in the agricultural business.

There are distinct advantages to constructing large, new barns. However, with this option comes greater risk. The entire crop could be lost if the new construction runs into difficulty. There would also be higher construction costs. Demolition, the increased square footage, and the structural requirements of a larger building all contribute to the increased cost. The risk in the bigger barns option is unquestionably greater, but so is the reward.

As a businessperson, I would like you to do as the landowner did in Jesus's parable. I want you to deliberate, to reason. I want you to consider all the available options and make the decision how to solve the problem of a harvest that exceeds storage capacity. The odds are that after you have weighed the options and calculated the risk versus reward, you would, like the rich landowner, decide to tear down the existing barns and build new, larger ones.

It is difficult for me to be critical of the landowner for having made what I consider to be a good business decision. Where is the fault in that? From a business perspective, he cannot be considered a fool. I would be guilty of the same. No doubt Robert would also have opted for larger barns. It is consistent with the direction that he chose for his own business. Believing in himself, he elected the course of greater risk aimed at the possibility of long-term returns.

There is yet another parallel between Robert and the landowner, a parallel most business owners and managers share.

> *And I will say to my soul, "Soul, you have many goods laid up for many years to come; take your ease, eat, drink and be merry."*
> **LUKE 12:19**

Make certain here that you do not misinterpret the meaning of the word *soul*. Although it includes our spiritual nature or the lack thereof, it is not just a spiritual entity. *The New International Dictionary of the Bible*[1] defines *soul* as "the word commonly used in the Bible to designate the non-material ego of man in its ordinary relationship with earthly and physical things." We commonly refer to it as our inner being or our nonphysical self.

If you recall in my contemporary parable, after landing the big contract, Robert's desire was to finally slow down, spend some time with his family, and enjoy life. After years of toiling, working long hours, rushing, planning, and sacrificing, Robert stood on the threshold of a renewed relationship with his wife and family. He was on the cusp of living comfortably off the fruits of his labor. Robert's conversation with himself in the cockpit of that airplane was the reconciliation of his inner self, the reconciliation of his soul. It was his inner being celebrating the fulfillment of his original intent when he took a chance and walked away from the security of his corporate job. That conversation was his soul replaying the struggles and sacrifices of the past while anticipating all the things those struggles had made possible.

If you have ever had one of these moments, you understand what I am talking about. You understand completely what Robert and the rich landowner were feeling. The emotion is both exhilarating and peaceful, all at the same time. The landowner's soul had that same conversation. Say what you will about this man's position and wealth, it evidently did not come without a cost, according to Scripture. It was not just handed to him. It did not come easy. Why would anyone anticipate the "taking of their ease for years to come" if they were

---

1. "Soul," New International Dictionary of the Bible (Grand Rapids, MI: Zondervan, 1967).

already enjoying that lifestyle? There is no need to anticipate what you are presently doing. You don't anticipate Christmas on Christmas Day, and you do not anticipate retirement if you have already retired. The landowner is looking forward to something that he has not yet been able to do. Read Luke 12:19 again.

> *And I will say to my soul, "Soul, you have many good things laid up for many years to come; take your ease, eat, drink and be merry."*
> **LUKE 12:19**

This reads as the anticipation of a man who has worked and made sacrifice to reach this rewarding point in life. The productive crop that was coming to harvest was going to allow the landowner to enjoy the fruits of his labor. Again, it is difficult for me to find fault in that, and hardly seems worthy of "fool." The expectation of the landowner actually appears to have scriptural parallel in the thoughts and words of Solomon.

> *So I commended pleasure, for there is nothing good for a man under the sun except to eat and to drink and to be merry, and this will stand by him in his toils throughout the days of his life which God has given him under the sun.*
> **ECCLESIASTES 8:15**

These are the stories of two men, each having taken risks, who worked hard and seemingly made good business decisions. They are both standing on the brink of great success and the opportunity to enjoy the fruits of their labor. Suddenly everything changes.

> *But God said to him, "You fool! This very*
> *night your soul is required of you."*
>
> **LUKE 12:20**

In my mind, I can see this landowner staring at the very spot where his new barns will stand as God delivers the shocking news. I can also envision Robert staring out the airplane windshield into the star-filled sky as he learns of his fate from the voice of Almighty God. In that message there is no need for deliberation, no need for reasoning, no need for an action plan. It has been decided. God's decision is final.

I stated earlier that two adjectives cause us to form our opinion of the landowner. The first is *rich*, and we have discussed it at length. The second is *fool*. Just as in the case of *rich*, I believe that within the context of this parable it is possible we are much too hasty and too harsh in our judgment of the landowner because of the word *fool*. There is no doubt that *fool* is an ominous description in Scripture. The term is used to describe a godless condition, and it is used quite often.

This is especially true in the book of Proverbs. The reason *fool* appears so often is that the Hebrew term for *proverb* means a "comparison." The book of Proverbs illustrates many comparisons between wisdom and foolishness. They are diametric opposites; foolishness is the absence of wisdom. What then is wisdom? Wisdom is the application of godly principles in life. Evil, godless people by their nature cannot help but engage in foolish behavior, but for someone to act foolishly does not automatically indicate that they are godless. Just as in the case of being rich, if foolishness were an automatic condemnation of a person's entire spiritual condition, many of us would be in trouble.

As Christians, we still have opportunities to do foolish things. It is an opportunity that I take advantage of on far too many occasions. I imagine you do the same. Indulging in our anger, selfishness, resentment, and vengeance are all identified as foolish behavior. You may be surprised by some of the examples found in Scripture.

> *Then Aaron said to Moses, "Oh, my lord, I beg you, do not account this sin to us, in which we have acted foolishly and in which we have sinned."*
> **NUMBERS 12:11**

Aaron's plea is made on behalf of God's chosen people. Later in the book of Deuteronomy, Moses spoke in the assembly of Israel, again addressing God's chosen.

> *Do you thus repay the Lord,*
> *O foolish and unwise people?*
> *Is He not your Father who has bought you?*
> *He has made you and established you.*
> **DEUTERONOMY 32:6**

The people who Moses is identifying as foolish and unwise have a "God the Father" relationship. They themselves are aware that they have been bought with a price. They are aware that God not only established them, but He also sustains them. These are not godless people.

Even David, the man that God proclaimed to be a "man after God's own heart" had his moments of foolishness. David's moments no doubt outweigh any of the things that most of us are guilty of, since his include adultery, deception, and ultimately murder.

> *David said to God, "I have sinned greatly, in that I have done this thing. But now, please take away the iniquity of Your servant, for I have done very foolishly."*
> **1 CHRONICLES 21:8**

We can even act foolish trying to do what we believe is the right thing. Look again at the father of the prodigal son. He certainly must have known the personality and nature of his children. At the time of this parable, they were young adults. From the conclusion of the parable, we know the father was a wise man. The younger son's lack of self-discipline, selfishness, and poor decision-making would have been evident to his father. Still, he agreed to the son's selfish request, knowing it was a decision that had the strong possibility of bringing about the young man's self-destruction. I would look at this and say the prodigal father made a much more foolish decision than building bigger barns.

What I would like you to consider is whether Jesus was condemning the rich landowner as "godless" or if He was describing his action as foolish, thereby making him a "fool." There is no other indication from the entire parable that would lead us to believe that the rich landowner was a godless man. Again, no mention of being evil or deceitful, no mention of maliciously gaining wealth through extortion or abuse, no mention of intentionally neglecting the things of God, nor any vile response to God's judgment.

After investigation of the Scripture, I tend to believe that it is very possible that the landowner was, in fact, a decent person, a hardworking businessman trying to make good business decisions, who ended up engaged in foolish behavior. It is very possible that he was not unlike Robert. The background of the rich landowner is one of the many questions I hope to ask God face-to-face in glory. You may or may not agree with my perspective on his character, but in the end it does not matter. Whether he was a greedy, godless, money-loving fool or just a godly businessman who fell into foolish behavior, the net result was the same. Standing on the threshold of his dynamic business achievement, he would not live to enjoy it.

Was it God's judgment for seeking possessions? Was it a form of punishment for what the landowner had done? Is it in response to the landowner's desire for greater profit? That does not seem to be consistent with Proverbs 14:23–24. We are not denied profit from our labor; quite the opposite actually. Profit is the expectation of labor.

> *In all labor there is profit,*
> *But mere talk leads only to poverty.*
> *The crown of the wise is their riches,*
> *But the folly of fools is foolishness.*
> **PROVERBS 14:23–24**

The issue does not appear to be the labor or the profit or even the accumulation of riches. Based upon the comprehensive context of Scripture, those are not punishable offenses. I do not believe Robert's sad fate or that of the rich landowner was a case of God's judgment. I do not believe the two men were punished by God with an early death. Their appointed time had been set long before the large contract or the productive crop.

What then is the message of these two parables?

They each ran out of time while focused on the pursuit of something that evidently had little significance to God. If God did have an interest, wouldn't He have allowed them to stick around long enough to see it to completion? That is where we err as believers. We want to make things that have no eternal value important. We pursue things that Scripture refers to as earthly treasures. Not the least of these treasures is our business. Because we place great significance upon it, we desire—or even expect—that God shares in that perspective and views it the same way.

Our businesses are earthly treasures. They hold no value in the eternal kingdom. God is not going to place importance upon them just because we do. The parables are not sad because two lives ended early. They are sad because so much of the time that they had been divinely allotted was spent focused on pursuits that had no eternal significance. Allow me to paraphrase and amplify Luke 12:20.

You fool! Could you not see that you were exhausting, squandering your time, your energy, your attention on something that has no eternal value? I have no use for your barns in heaven, and when you are gone, you will have no use for them on earth. Now your time is up. Your one short trip across this wonderful creation, earth, is over, and what you thought you had gained amounts to nothing. Such a waste, such a foolish waste.

It is not that God dislikes business; that is not the case. Business is neither good nor bad in God's sight; it is neutral, the same as money. Few who understand Scripture would argue with the fact that money itself is neither good nor bad. Rather, our attitude toward it and use of it is what holds God's interest. It can be a useful tool or a deadly weapon. The same is true of your business. It is not the business that holds God's interest, but rather you, operating within the business. We do not ask God to bless our money, but yet we feel it necessary to ask that blessing upon our business. On an eternal scale, is there a discernible difference between the two?

I recall many years ago, my wife and I purchased some property and built a new house. It was (at least for its time and our young age) a very nice house. It was certainly much larger and more impressive than anything my grandmother had ever lived in. I was extremely proud of the house. For me it was a symbol of our hard work, a visible sign of what Lisa and I had been able to accomplish at a young age. I knew that Grandma would be impressed, and although she lived eight hundred miles away, I wanted very badly for her to see it in person.

Some months after we had moved in, she came to visit. As we rode up the driveway, I expected some kind of comment about how splendid a place we had built. Instead, she continued to inquire about our family. We walked inside and still no comment about the house, her eyes riveted to her two great-grandsons playing on the floor. In that moment, it occurred to me that our handsome stack of wood and bricks meant very little to her even though she had never owned anything its equal. The only thing that mattered to her at our address was the people who lived there.

God has no interest in our business plan, our five-year growth projections, our market share, or the size of our warehouse. He does not concern Himself with them. He only concerns Himself with me. It is me He chooses to love, and in so doing, it is me He chooses to bless or chastise. It is me He desires to maintain and grow a relationship with. It is me whose days He has numbered and who wants those days used to their greatest eternal potential.

Our businesses are earthly treasures. They hold no eternal value. God is not going to place importance upon them just because we do. That is a fallacy. It is false teaching that has no biblical support. God does not bend His value system to match the ones that we concoct. We must learn to bend our value system to match His. To me, that is the spiritual truth, as well as the great business message in the bigger barns parable.

It would be folly, great foolishness if I reach the end of my appointed time upon this earth—whether that be in thirty years or thirty minutes—and the operation, growth, and success of my business has been given the best of my life.

> *Come now, you who say, "Today or tomorrow we shall go to such and such a city, and spend a year there and engage in business and make a profit." Yet you do not know what your life will be like tomorrow. You are just a vapor that appears for a little while and then vanishes away.*
>
> **JAMES 4:13–14**

CHAPTER 3

WHAT DO YOU WANT?

My dad had a unique sense of humor. If he needed to run an errand while any of his young grandchildren were visiting his house, he would tell them that he was going to the pony store. Dad would ask if anyone wanted him to pick up a pony for them while he was there. The first couple times, the grandkids would get excited. Who wouldn't want a pony? He would ask their color preference and head to town. When dad came back without a pony, he'd tell them the pony store was out of the color they had requested. Some might think it cruel, but not those of us who understood dad's humor. It did not take long for the grandkids to figure out that there was no pony store and all their requests stopped.

Well, almost all their requests stopped. I have one nephew whose customary response became, "I know there is not a pony store, but if there is, I want a brown one." Each time he was asked, he placed his order for a brown pony on the outside chance that there might really be such a place. You could just see his little mind wrangling with how tragic it would be if he did not get a brown pony just because he did not ask for it.

"I still do not understand why you have such a problem with asking God to bless our business. Even if you don't think business matters to Him, it doesn't hurt to ask."

When my wife said this to me, the pony store immediately came to mind. It seemed to me that her concern was that there was the possibility, or even worse the probability, that we might be missing out on some business blessings because I was not openly soliciting them. Before I had given her the opportunity to explain what she meant, I blurted out, "I know there's not a pony store, but if there is I'll take a brown one."

My sarcasm was uncalled for and way off the mark. Did I mention that I struggle with random moments of foolish behavior? Fortunately for me, she did not understand what I was saying. Unfortunately for me, I figured out what she was saying. Her concern had nothing to do with us not missing out on an outside chance. Hers was not, nor had it ever been, a "just in case" prayer. Shame on me for casting such a shallow viewpoint upon my wife.

Lisa has a spiritual depth that I cannot reach. It is quiet, humble, and usually on point. Her concern was that my aversion to praying for God to bless our business was the product of arrogance and pride. She was troubled by a suspicion that I had acquired an attitude of self-sufficiency and therefore felt that I had no need for divine assistance. At first, I was angry, upset that she could entertain such an idea. Then anger gave way to humility, and humility to shame. Somewhere within my words or actions I must have left an indication, or at least a trace, of smug self-regard. I understand where her concern comes from.

The business community reveres the moniker "self-made." It is easy to get wrapped up in the whole "built something from nothing" mentality. Arrogance and pride are large players in business, and success is the fuel that feeds them. I am mindful of that trap. I take pride in my efforts, but I am not arrogant enough to think that I have no need for God during the workday. I understand my continual need for wisdom and my dependence upon God's provision.

If I honestly believed that by supplication I could win His favor in business, I would spend most of the day in specific prayer. The stakes are high. Failure would destroy us financially. The bank holds liens against all our major assets. I know I am fallible and that there is a whole lot about operating a business that I have yet to learn. I know I do not have all the answers, and I know I am capable of failure. If divine assistance is available for business, simply by asking for it, the line is going to have to form behind me.

I was not struggling with whether or not I had a need for God's blessings; I was struggling with the form of that need. I will gladly, gratefully, and humbly accept all the help, favor, and blessings that God is willing to bestow, but I just cannot find scriptural evidence to support the belief that God cares about business.

The immediate response from most Christians is that God cares about everything that causes us concern, and the Scripture that is most often cited in support of that response is found in 1 Peter.

> *Therefore humble yourselves under the mighty hand of God, that He may exalt you at the proper time, casting all your anxiety on Him, because He cares for you.*
> **1 PETER 5:6–7**

The word *all* in this verse would certainly seem to be inclusive of business, and therefore business falls under the umbrella of God's care, right? There are two problems with that supposition. The first is the nature of those things that He invites us to cast upon Him. Peter calls upon us to cast our "anxiety" upon the Lord. To better understand what he is referring to, we need to refer to Jesus's instructions on the topic of anxiety.

> *No one can serve two masters; for either he will hate the one and love the other, or he will be devoted to one and despise the other. You cannot serve God and wealth. For this reason I say to you, do not be worried about your life, as to what you will eat, or what you should drink; nor for your body, as to what you will eat or what you will drink; nor for your body, as to what you will put on. Is not life more than food, and the body more than clothing?... For the Gentiles eagerly seek all these things; for your heavenly Father knows that you need all these things. But seek first His kingdom and His righteousness, and all these things will be added to you. So do not worry about tomorrow; for tomorrow will care for itself. Each day has enough trouble of its own.*
>
> **MATTHEW 6:24–25; 32–34**

In the book of 1 Peter, we are instructed to cast all our anxiety upon God, and yet in the Gospel of Matthew, we are instructed by Jesus to be anxious for nothing. How do we reconcile these two? I believe the answer lies in the full context. In the Gospel of Matthew, Jesus is clearly addressing our concern over being able to satisfy all our physical needs. This would also include our concern over the "wants" that are in excess of our needs. Paraphrased, His instruction is:

God knows that you have physical needs, and He will help you meet them. Do not be so overly concerned about those needs that they cause you anxiety.

That is not the same as Peter's instruction. In the book of 1 Peter the context of "casting all of your anxiety upon Him" is entirely different. This verse is not surrounded by our physical needs; it is part of an exhortation regarding spiritual service. When you look at excerpts from 1 Peter 5:1–10, it is evident that the anxieties that Peter is inviting us to cast upon God are those associated with the struggles and challenges that are part of serving His kingdom.

> *Therefore, I exhort the elders among you ... shepherd the flock of God among you, exercising oversight not under compulsion, but voluntarily, according to the will of God; and not for sordid gain, but with eagerness; ... proving to be examples to the flock ... You younger men, likewise, be subject to your elders; and all of you, clothe yourselves with humility toward one another.*
>
> **1 PETER 5:1–3, 5**

It is at this point that the focal passage, the "cast all your anxiety" verse appears. Clearly, up to this point, Peter is not addressing concerns over meeting our physical needs. Let's continue.

> *Be of sober spirit, be on the alert. Your adversary, the devil, prowls around like a roaring lion, seeking someone to devour. But resist him, firm in your faith ... And after you have suffered for a little while, the God of all grace, who called you to His eternal glory in Christ, will Himself perfect, confirm, strengthen and establish you.*
>
> **1 PETER 5:8–10**

There can be no mistake that when taken within context, these two passages regarding anxiety are addressing different circumstances. The passage in Matthew concerns anxiety over physical need, and Jesus instructs us not to allow ourselves to be anxious for those things. Peter's exhortation concerns anxiety over spiritual service, and he invites us to cast all those anxieties upon a caring God. The question we must ask ourselves is: which of these two passages applies to the concerns or anxieties we have over our business?

When we petition God to "bless our business," what are we honestly asking Him to do? What is it that we want to see come about as a result of our request? Are we looking for growth or expansion of our facilities? Do we want increased sales, to improve our market share? Perhaps sales are good, but we need increased profitability. Do we hope that our request manifests itself in the form of greater margins or operating capital?

When I think of the things that are necessary for the continued operation and growth of our business, these are the type of things that come to my mind. I dare say that as a businessman, I am not alone. These are all critical elements of survival in the business world. Christian or not, as a business owner or manager, you must also have needs and desires along the same line. Are these the outcomes we hope to receive as we ask God, in prayer, to bless our business?

My honest answer would have to be yes. There may be rare exceptions, but the truth is that our plea for God to bless our business typically boils down to a request for financial gain. The dilemma I am faced with is this: Does my request, delivered to God as a "care that I am casting upon Him," align more closely with the anxiety over physical need in Matthew that I should not have or anxiety over a spiritual need that Peter says God desires to take upon Himself? If it falls into the category of physical need or want, the question now becomes: Does God desire to further bless me financially? Does He want me to have more? Even more importantly, does He want me to have a concern over having more?

We have already looked at multiple Scripture verses regarding God's view of wealth. Jesus and His apostles spent a great deal of time addressing the love of, pursuit of, influence of, correct use of, and potential danger of money. It is hard to ignore all the warnings.

So, we must ask ourselves, knowing full well the range of problems money can present and the negative potential it holds, does God desire to further bless us financially in business? The other question we must consider is do we truly want Him to increase our wealth?

Remember the parable of the prodigal son? The father in this story, whom we identify as a "good" wealthy landowner, employed both of his sons in the family business. Although it required labor on their part, each of his sons had a good life and presumably a secure future. Neither of them had any need to be anxious regarding their physical needs. Even so, the younger son desired more. He asked his father to give him the portion of his inheritance that was deserved.

> *The younger of them said to his father, "Father, give me the share of the estate that falls to me." So he divided his wealth between them.*
>
> **LUKE 15:12**

Being a father myself, I believe the younger son's request hurt the father. It had to. What loving, caring father would not be hurt? He had provided his child with all the necessities of life. His children did not want for food, clothing, and shelter. Beyond the basic necessities, the son had also enjoyed some of life's luxuries, and the father's estate would provide a secure future. But the abundance was still not enough to satisfy his child. He requested more. The words of the young son must have stung the ears and broke the heart of his father. I am certain that it was with hesitation and sadness that the father acquiesced. Scripture tells us in Luke 15:13 that "not many days later," the younger son gathered up his things and left town. We all know from our knowledge of Scripture that in Luke 15:14–16, the son squanders the inheritance that he was given and finds himself in a much worse condition than he was in while working in his father's business.

> *Now when he had spent everything, a severe famine occurred in that country, and he began to be impoverished. So he went and hired himself out to one of the citizens of that country, and he sent him into his fields to feed swine. And he would have gladly filled his stomach with the pods that the swine were eating, and no one was giving anything to him.*
>
> **LUKE 15:14–16**

In short, the prodigal son was given exactly what he had asked for, and it ruined him. As businessmen we choose not to identify with the young man's plight. We imagine ourselves to be so much different than the son. We imagine ourselves to be much better able to discipline ourselves and control our desires. There is no way that we, being given the things we ask for, would put ourselves in a similar situation.

We refuse to believe that we could bring about our own ruin even though that same scenario is continually played out around us. The very thing we so earnestly desire becomes the instrument of our demise. Certain that more is good and bigger is better, we pray for these things in our business life. Once received, they sadden, or in some cases ruin, our lives. It was what the apostle Paul described to Timothy as having "pierced themselves through with many sorrows" (1 Timothy 6:10, KJV).

Those sorrows are not limited to financial matters. Sorrows manifest themselves in many different forms. A shift in values, erosion of work ethic, neglected relationships, an ungrateful attitude, and destructive habits are just some examples of the many pangs.

In my own life, I have seen good men, godly men, men who no doubt prayed for the success of their business end up in anguish. Their businesses grew and expanded quickly. Their prayers for God's blessing seemed to have been heard, and yet as time passed, I watched as the burden of their increase crushed what had been an otherwise stable business. Businesses have been ruined, families torn apart, personal health destroyed, and spiritual concerns forsaken, all as a result of the blessing of "more."

Was it a case of God reversing His decision? Did He answer the prayer for more and then retract the blessing? I don't think so. Perhaps, as in the parable of the prodigal son, God reluctantly honored the request of one of His children even though He knew the damage it could cause.

Ask yourself: When I pray for God to bless my business, what am I truly requesting? Then ask yourself: Am I requesting something that God desires me to have? If you are focused upon financial increase when you ask for God's blessing, the overwhelming probability is that you are on your own.

Do not weary yourself to gain wealth,
Cease from your consideration of it.

> *When you set your eyes on it, it is gone.*
> *For wealth certainly makes itself wings*
> *Like an eagle that flies toward the heavens.*
>
> **PROVERBS 23:4–5**

> *Better is a dry morsel and quietness with it*
> *Than a house full of feasting with strife.*
>
> **PROVERBS 17:1**

> *But those who want to get rich fall into temptation*
> *and a snare and many foolish and harmful desires*
> *which plunge men into ruin and destruction.*
>
> **1 TIMOTHY 6:9**

The list of possible side effects would seem to be enough to discourage a loving father from obliging. Stress, fatigue, frustration, and calamity are just the short list. However, the truth is that God will oblige the misguided request of a hardheaded believer.

I am reminded of the nation of Israel's request for a king to rule over them. The request is recorded in 1 Samuel 8. Samuel served as judge over Israel until his old age. He then appointed his sons as judges over Israel. The sons were not cut from the same cloth as their father and proved to be, at best, unethical, taking bribes and perverting justice. The elders were upset and asked Samuel to appoint a king to rule over the people. Neither Samuel nor God was pleased with the request for a king. God told His servant Samuel to warn the people of Israel about the negative consequences of appointing a king.

> *"Now then, listen to their voice; however, you shall solemnly*
> *warn them and tell them of the procedure of the king who*

> *will reign over them." So Samuel spoke all the words of the Lord to the people who had asked of him a king. He said, "This will be the procedure of the king who will reign over you: he will take your sons and place them for himself in his chariots and among his horsemen and they will run before his chariots. He will appoint for himself commanders of thousands and of fifties, and some to do his plowing and to reap his harvest and to make his weapons of war and equipment for his chariots. He will also take your daughters for perfumers and cooks and bakers. He will take the best of your fields and your vineyards and your olive groves and give them to his servants. He will take a tenth of your seed and of your vineyards and give to his officers and to his servants. He will also take your male servants and your female servants and your best young men and your donkeys and use them for his work. He will take a tenth of your flocks, and you yourselves will become his servants. Then you will cry out in that day because of your king whom you have chosen for yourselves, but the Lord will not answer you in that day."*
>
> **1 SAMUEL 8:9–18**

The Lord, through His servant Samuel, delivers a very stern warning to the people of Israel. The consequences of their request for a king are incredibly dire. The list of lost possessions, broken relationships, and forced labor is staggering. I have made some bad deals in my life and I have entered into some regrettable contracts, but never have I agreed to anything like this. Who would say yes to this deal? The nation of Israel, that's who.

> *Nevertheless, the people refused to listen to the voice of Samuel, and they said, "No, but there shall be a king over us, that we also may be like all the nations, that our king may judge us and go out before us and fight our battles."*
>
> **1 SAMUEL 8:19–20**

We look at their decision and say that it is absurd. The Lord told them of the hazards, the misery, the suffering, and the tumult that will become part of their life if He honors their request for a king, and still, they insist on a king. It is complete and utter foolishness, right?

In reality, it is not that different from what we do on a regular basis ourselves, when financial gain is the motivation behind our request for God's blessing upon our business. Repeatedly, Scripture delivers warnings regarding the accumulation of wealth and the danger of continually seeking increase. We are warned about the stress, the frustration, the weariness, and the bitterness that can accompany the pursuit of riches. We are warned of the possibility of bringing about our own destruction. Yet, just like the people of Israel, we say, nevertheless, it is what we want. I truly believe that God will, at that time, honor a request that is not in our best interest, and like the nation of Israel and the prodigal son, we suffer the consequences.

I am not suggesting, and more importantly, God is not declaring, that success in business will lead to destruction. There are motives other than financial gain that people have for seeking God's favor on their business. We have throughout history, and in our contemporary culture, seen examples of successful businesses that were built and run by virtuous people. Examined honestly, I believe them to be a small percentage—in fact, a rarity.

I don't intend that to be a spiritual criticism; it is simply a reflection of the personality type and mindset of an entrepreneur. They think in terms of growth. They increase, expand, and innovate. Though it makes them no better or no worse than the rest of society, it does delineate them. It is the way that business owners and business builders are wired. To criticize them for possessing that mindset is akin to berating a dog for wagging his tail. Scripture does not condemn success in business, but it makes abundantly clear that along with success comes a heightened potential for misery.

So, it is possible that our prayers for increase in business are a request for something that God does not see as drawing us nearer to the virtues that He would prefer we possess. I confess that in my own life, my business eye focuses primarily on growth and increase. It may glance in the direction of more virtuous gain but always seems to return its focus to monetary concerns.

At this point in my spiritual and professional life, I am not yet one of those rare exceptions. Any attempt to disguise that fact in a cloak of spiritual motivation may deceive some people, but neither God nor I are fooled.

So, what then does my prayer for God's blessing actually sound like in His ear? What does your prayer for business blessings sound like in His ear? Before you offer up that prayer for your business, honestly answer this question:

When I ask God to bless my business, what am I specifically requesting, and is my request consistent with the things that matter to Him? Are the cares and anxieties that we have in business the type that the apostle Peter encourages us to cast upon God, or are they more in line with the type that Jesus says we should not possess?

CHAPTER 4

FRACTIONS

By itself, the bigger barns parable does not comprehensively substantiate my belief that God does not care about business, but coupled with the things that Scripture teaches God does concern Himself with, the argument becomes more compelling. Even so, I understand that there are still many who, like my wife, require more. As we continue to investigate, I believe that Scripture will oblige, but first I want to ask another question.

As Christians, how do we biblically reconcile the fact that the businesses of some very godly people fail, while other businesses, owned by people with no spiritual regard, succeed?

I cannot cite any data that suggests Christian businesses have a greater success rate than non-Christian businesses. Even more confounding to me than the believer versus nonbeliever issue is the inequity between one Christian business and another. Why does one succeed while the other fails? Is God blessing some while deliberately ignoring others? Is He picking and choosing from among those who are asking? If so, what are the criteria for finding God's favor? How can I get my prayers for blessing to the top of the list? How does my prayer for help in business gain precedence over someone else?

Is it a spiritual contest? Hopefully not, or I may be in more trouble than I thought.

We are amused at the notion that prior to an athletic contest, opposing team members each pray to the same God for victory. It seems spiritually immature, but it is not limited to just young people. Who among us has not seen grown men or women, hands clasped, heads bowed in prayer, on the sideline at some pivotal point in the game, no doubt asking God to grant them favor? Is God inclined to choose one team's prayer over the others, or does He leave the outcome in the hands of those competing? In our learned faith, it seems to be a silly question. We are quite certain that the God of the universe does not dabble in the outcome of contests.

How different are the prayers of those athletes from those of businessmen? God does not tilt the playing field at the bequest of players or fans, and I find it unlikely that He tilts the boardroom in answer to prayer. It is especially true of prayers that target being awarded a contract over a business competitor. Why would I say that? It is the product of many years of observation. When I look around at the varying fates of Christian enterprise, I am unable to make a connection between spiritual depth and business success. Can you?

In the absence of visible spiritual justification for the success of some and failure of others, we must reach one of two conclusions. Either it is God's specific will that some businesses succeed while others fail regardless of spiritual depth (in which case, prayers are going to be of no use anyway), or it is not God's desire to be involved in the success or failure of business.

As believers, it is an "either/or" that we really don't like, so we have created a popular compromise theory. If we succeed, it is by God's blessing, and if we fail, it is our own doing. The problem is that this theory is biblically unsupported. Without question, an abundance of Scripture warns us of the consequences of disobedience or poor judgment. The things we do, the actions we take, and the attitudes we possess can bring about our own demise, which is true not only in business but in life. However, the opposite is also true. Scripture makes it clear that we contribute greatly to our own success.

> *Poor is he who works with a negligent hand,*
> *But the hand of the diligent makes rich.*
>
> **PROVERBS 10:4**

> *The plans of the diligent lead surely to advantage,*
> *But everyone who is hasty comes surely to poverty.*
>
> **PROVERBS 21:5**

> *Do you see a man skilled in his work?*
> *He will stand before kings;*
> *He will not stand before obscure men.*
>
> **PROVERBS 22:29**

I have enormous respect for the late Truett Cathy and the wildly successful business that he founded, Chick-fil-A. Throughout the world there may be many small businesses that are similarly operated, but in the corporate world, he was an anomaly. His son, Dan, continued in his father's footsteps. Truett Cathy was a model of humility, exercising wisdom, and consistency in his Christian walk. In addition, he was a brilliant businessman, and for that he does not get near enough credit. Christians tend to attribute all his business success to his relationship to Christ, when in fact his success in business is due to him being a very good businessman.

Make no mistake, Mr. Cathy was a trophy of the Almighty and a very blessed man, but the success of Chick-fil-A is a product of high-quality, delicious food, the friendliest and most respectful workforce in the industry, spotless dining rooms, clean restrooms, well-maintained storefronts, and disciplined growth. If Chick-fil-A had poor quality food, dirty restrooms, or unfriendly associates, it does not matter how closely Mr. Cathy walked with God, his business would have failed. That is a critical element of this study, and it compels me to ask some questions.

Is it possible that a godly business can fail because the owner is simply not a good businessman? The Scriptures listed above seem to indicate it is possible. Can it fail because of economic circumstance beyond the owner's control? Can a business fail due to poor decisions made by a person who is spiritually well-grounded? Can it fail amid prayers for God to bless it? Yes, yes, yes, and yes. It can, and it has. All these questions, and their obvious answers, point to the conclusion that the success or failure of a business depends more upon the proprietor's effort, ability, and ingenuity than their spiritual posture. Otherwise, how are we able to account for the conflicting results?

Where does that leave us? It is ridiculous to suggest that God ignores or abandons us while we are conducting business. I can certainly agree with my wife in that regard. We are no less the children of God in the office than we are in the church. To gain understanding of how God interacts with the business world, we need to view it from His perspective.

The rich and the poor have a common bond,
The Lord is the maker of them all.

PROVERBS 22:2

This is rarely seen as a business verse, but I challenge you to view it in that light. In Proverbs 22:2 a clear line is being drawn regarding how people are viewed. On one side of that line is our physical net worth: "the rich and the poor." If you think of it as a fraction, this value is the numerator. It is the side of the line where the sum of our assets is tallied. Accounting balance sheets refer to it as net worth. Flesh and blood are given a monetary value. On this side of the line, the numerator, each of us has a numeric value that falls somewhere between rich and poor.

The other side of the line is where we find our spiritual worth. We will call it the denominator. From God's perspective, we are all viewed the same. Each of us is loved and worth dying to save. The denominator represents a bond, a love relationship that is dependent upon nothing else. On this side of the line, nothing that is monetary has any value. In fact, Scripture points to the fact that the denominator is common, for "the Lord is the maker of them all." When you think about it, we are all metaphoric fractions, each possessing a unique numerator and a common denominator. I believe Proverbs 22:2 does not just delineate between the monetary and the spiritual, it helps us to better understand where God places His focus.

The first question I asked myself was: Why did God feel it necessary to make such a declaration? What was His purpose? He has taken the two opposite ends of the socioeconomic spectrum and formed a connection between them. Truthfully, He has formed more than a connection. God has declared them bound by a common truth. Why?

I believe His intent is to bring clarity to our differences in perception, to bring clarity to the way He views us as opposed to the way we normally view ourselves. Among ourselves, we tend to focus primarily on the value of the numerator, while He is clearly much more interested in the denominator. While we are measuring each other on a monetary scale of rich to poor, He is measuring on a completely different scale. It is a difference that God felt was worth addressing in Proverbs 22:2.

The numerator — the monetary value placed upon us — is largely due to our own efforts. It is the product of our own hands, our own minds. I can hear the gasps, the whispers of heresy. How dare I utter such blasphemy! I can hear the retort, "Everything we are, everything we have, or hope to have, is by God's omnipotent hand." Get over it. If that were the case, there would be no need for Scripture regarding diligence or the work of skilled hands. There would be no need for Scripture to admonish slothfulness. No need to be encouraged to "do all things, as unto the Lord."

We have been wonderfully, skillfully, imaginatively made. The human brain by itself is an incredible, complex, almost unexplainable organ. I find it amusingly ironic that the scientific and engineering community is fixated upon trying to produce an electromechanical equivalent to the very organ that makes their efforts possible. God constructed us in this fashion for a reason. We were given the ability to think, to reason, to imagine, and to create. Within that God-given ability, we make decisions, we act, we react, we respond. It is the most wonderful element of our design and the motivation behind God's creation of man.

> *Then God said, "Let Us make man in Our image, according to Our likeness."*
> **GENESIS 1:26**

That likeness is spirit, mind, emotion, and will, and it was given to us for a purpose. God gave humans dominion. We are doers, created in God's own image. We have been given by our very design, the physical and intellectual tools for taking action. With that capability came the obligation to use those tools. It is a divine expectation that is creation based. We are designed with the ability to pursue those things that satisfy the likeness we possess, to pursue the things that satisfy the spirit and the mind.

Oftentimes we Christians do not seize the role of doers and we surrender our influence. We do not fulfill our obligations and therefore forfeit blessings by misinterpreting God's gifts. His gifts are not "all the things that we have, or ever hope to have," as some might argue. God's gifts are unique to Him. They are the gifts that cannot be given by anyone else. We have reversed the intended meaning of Scripture to the point of attributing things to God that He does not want credit for.

> *Every good and perfect gift is from above, coming down from the Father of the heavenly lights, who does not change like shifting shadows.*
> **JAMES 1:17**, NIV

Yes, God is the giver of every good and perfect gift, but there are conflicting ideas of what constitutes "good" and "perfect." Some of the things that we try to include under the umbrella of this Scripture simply do not apply. We possess things that do not satisfy God's definition of good. Our businesses seem to be among them. Though it is neither intentional nor egregious, when we misinterpret the gifts that James 1:17 is referring to, we create two problems in our business life.

First, we diminish the significance of our divinely conceived design when we include the fruits of our labor in the category of "every good and perfect gift." God had a purpose in creating us in His likeness.

There was a purpose in designing us to be thinkers and doers. The blueprint included mind, spirit, and free will. Individual will is the very thing that makes our obedience so endearing to God. The fruit of our labor is the product of our own hands, our minds, and our will. Scripture makes it very clear.

> *When you shall eat of the fruit of your hands, You will be happy and it will be well with you.*
>
> **PSALM 128:2**

The gift is not what is produced by the labor. The "good and perfect gifts" are the physical and mental capacity to do the labor, along with God-given environmental elements that sustain the potential for labor. They are the gifts that can only be given by the "Father of heavenly lights." When Scripture referred to God as the "Father of heavenly lights," the reference was to all forms of light: spiritual, physical, intellectual, and moral. The plan is for us to use all of the "good and perfect gifts" to provide for ourselves.

Let's look at a simple example. Since we are referencing the Scripture regarding fruit, we will use produce as the example. Let's say that I own a farm. I have planted and nurtured my crop. I tend to it throughout the year, cultivating, fertilizing, and watering as necessary. The "good and perfect gifts" are my ability to do the work and the intellect to understand what is required. The soil, the sunshine, and the rain that sustained the growth of the crops are also gifts from God. At harvest time, I pick my field and prepare it for market, where it will produce an income. That income is the fruit of my labor. It came about only because I chose to make use of the "good and perfect gifts." For that reason, I do not agree with the "everything that we have, and everything that we hope to have is by God's hand" mentality. It negates God's design intent in making "man in Our own image."

Whether or not it was intentional, Chick-fil-A has incorporated this very principle in one of their advertising slogans. For that reason, it is one of my favorite advertising campaigns.

"We didn't invent the chicken, just the chicken sandwich."

The chicken was, of course, God's invention. It was part of the world God created for man to inhabit. It is therefore included among the good and perfect gifts. On the other hand, that delicious chicken sandwich was Mr. Cathy's invention, the work of his mind, his hands, his imagination, his creativity, his insight. Even though I may think the sandwich is good—perhaps even perfect—it is not one of the good and perfect gifts.

We are designed with the mental and physical capacity to provide for ourselves from the bounty of God's creation. I will forever give God thanks for all His good and perfect gifts, but I will also give Him thanks for creating me with the capacity to apply them in order to generate an income for myself.

The second problem that is created by including the work of our hands, our assets, our businesses in the category of God's "good and perfect gifts" is distorted priorities. Although few owners literally want to turn their business over to God, our hope is that by casually attributing it to Him, we can give it an otherwise undeserved importance. If we place a cloak of spiritual significance over our monetary endeavors, there is no reason not to give those endeavors our fullest attention. We want the numerator in our metaphorical human fraction to be a spiritual matter, but it is not. The reality is that the numerator is largely the product of our own hands. It is a numeric value somewhere between rich and poor, equaling the worth of our accumulated possessions. Based upon Scripture, it would be difficult to define those possessions, including our businesses, as God's "good and perfect gifts."

The value of the numerator—our physical net worth—is typically the focal point as we view each other. It is how we measure worth and success. That is not the case with God. His interest lies in the denominator—where we are all loved in His eyes. Our financial net worth does not impress Him. Likewise, our lack of financial worth does not concern Him. God only seems concerned with the numerator when it has an impact upon the denominator. The problem is that, along with our free will and the mental capacity to produce, we also have the capacity to choose. We have the ability to determine, to reason, to choose what we are willing to sacrifice in pursuit of a greater net worth. When we are willing to disregard the denominator in pursuit of the numerator, God becomes concerned. It is for this reason I believe God made His declaration in Proverbs 22:2.

> *The rich and the poor have a common bond,*
> *The Lord is the maker of them all.*
> **PROVERBS 22:2**

When we read this verse, we focus on the "the rich and the poor," but what matters to God is the common bond, the second part of the verse. "The Lord is the maker of them all" takes us all the way back to the beginning. In fact, it takes us back to two beginnings: the beginning of time and the beginning of you, personally.

By the fifth day of creation, God had already put together an impressive portfolio of creation feats. He had created a universe so large that the human mind cannot grasp it, matter so small we cannot define it, and an earth so beautiful we cannot reproduce it. He had done some incredibly amazing things using only His breath, yet it was not enough to satisfy Him. God wanted more. He wanted a connection to creation. Something that could appreciate what had been done, while acknowledging the One who had done it. He desired spiritual, intellectual, and emotional interaction. Do not underestimate the Almighty God's desire to interact. Remember when Jesus was making His triumphant return to Jerusalem and the people were crying out in worship?

> *As soon as He was approaching, near the descent of the Mount of Olives, the whole crowd of the disciples began to praise God joyfully with a loud voice for all the miracles which they had seen, shouting:*
>
> "BLESSED IS THE KING WHO COMES
> IN THE NAME OF THE LORD;
>
> *Peace in heaven and glory in the highest!"*
> *Some of the Pharisees in the crowd said to Him, "Teacher, rebuke Your disciples." But Jesus answered, "I tell you, if these become silent, the stones will cry out!"*
>
> **LUKE 19:37–40**

God so desires this spiritual, intellectual, and emotional connection with His creation that if man fails in the task, He will go so far as to transfer that ability to rocks. Beware. Willfully forfeit the interaction element of your design intent and you can be replaced by a rock!

God designed and created us for the purpose of interaction. He wanted a connection. God's motivation for creating humans was fellowship with something in His own likeness. He still has that same desire. Despite everything we have done over the ages to spoil it, humanity continues to be the crown jewel of creation. We are mortal, flesh and blood shells that house a spirit God is able to communicate and fellowship with. In the likeness of God, we have a distinct purpose.

That was the first beginning. The second beginning was yours and mine. Like the billions that have come and gone before us, each of us has been individually created with that same purpose. God's primary desire and intent in your existence is that He may have fellowship with you, to have an interactive relationship with you. Rich or poor, young or old, male or female, black, white, and all shades in between, the Lord is Maker of them all, and each has been created for the same purpose. That is our common denominator, and it is where God places His focus.

Understanding the two opposing perspectives of the metaphorical human fraction, we are now able to interpret Proverbs 22:2 in relation to business. Our business is not one of the "good and perfect" gifts. It is the work of human hands. Business is what we produced from the good and perfect gifts that we were given.

In the grand scheme, in the eternal scope, our businesses themselves are neither good nor perfect. In fact, if we look at it candidly, they fall into the category of "earthly treasure"—the very treasure that Jesus said in Matthew 6:19 would be destroyed by moths and rust. A business is an earthly treasure. Where in Scripture are we encouraged to ask God to bless our earthly treasures? That does not mean that business is inherently evil. It just means it is not a priority with God. He concerns Himself with eternal treasure, treasures that can be stored in heaven, treasures that cannot be lost or destroyed.

Our efforts in business are directed at the numerator, the finances.

That is how business works. It is not ungodly; it's just how business succeeds. We use our God-given abilities to labor. If we work hard (or "diligently," as Scripture says), if we apply knowledge and wisdom, we have the potential to grow our net worth. We have the ability and the scriptural freedom to increase the value of our numerator. It is important to us, but God is neutral with regard to value of the numerator. He only has two expectations for this side of the human fraction. Both involve our work life, and each is important because each has a direct impact upon our relationship with Him. He may be neutral regarding the numerator, but when we start affecting the denominator, we draw God's attention.

Based upon Scripture, God expects that we will be willing to work to provide for our basic needs and the needs of our family.

> *For even when we were with you, we used to give you this order: if anyone is not willing to work, then he is not to eat, either.*
>
> **2 THESSALONIANS 3:10**

> *But if anyone does not provide for his own, and especially for those of his household, he has denied the faith and is worse than an unbeliever.*
>
> **1 TIMOTHY 5:8**

It is evident that God expects us to use the likeness we were created in and the environment we were placed in to provide for ourselves and our households. There can be no argument. God does not consider these things to be spiritual birthrights, freely and liberally poured out. Our basic needs are earned. They are earned through the thoughtful and diligent application of the good and perfect gifts.

If we are unwilling to do these things, we are acting in disobedience and have negatively impacted our relationship with God. We have tainted the denominator.

On the other end of the spectrum—yet equally important—if the work of our hands is able to produce beyond the basic needs, we face a different danger. Although God is neutral regarding your financial net worth, His eye is constantly on the denominator. If the actions we take and the attitudes we possess in pursuit of an increased numerator lead us into disobedience and erode our relationship, "the Maker of them all" becomes concerned. There are a lot of different ways for erosion to occur, and we will investigate them in greater detail in later chapters, but for now it is important just to understand how God views business.

By God's incredible design, we have been created with the ability, the freedom, and the expectation to provide for ourselves and our families. However, we have not been given the license to do so at the expense of divine obedience. God holds just two expectations for us in business. Neither of them has to do with annual sales, profit margins, growth projections, or market shares. Prayers for business that fall outside the boundaries of God's expectations would seem to fall on deaf ears. Prayers to bless the things that moths eat and rust destroys have no scriptural foundation. In fact, they are contrary to the way that Jesus taught us to pray. When asked by His disciples to teach them how to pray, Jesus responded by teaching them what is commonly known as the Lord's prayer, found in Matthew 6:9–13. The model for prayer that Jesus gave them began and ended with worship and exaltation. In between, just three requests were made:

1. The opportunity and ability to satisfy our most basic daily needs

2. Forgiveness for our transgressions (unfortunately, commensurate with their own willingness to forgive)

3. Rescue from evil

Jesus's model for prayer never touched upon the topic of our extended financial plans or the protection of our assets. Why?

I must believe that He did not see it as a significant element of our relationship with God. Should we see it as significant? When I think about how little time I actually spend in sincere, heartfelt prayer relative to all of my other daily activities, it seems offensive for me to spend even a moment asking for my earthly treasure to be blessed.

CHAPTER 5

DANGEROUS TERRITORY

I mentioned in an earlier chapter that there are reasons other than financial gain for seeking God's favor upon your business. I also stated that these are rare cases, the exception rather than the rule. The most common of these exceptions is ministry. There are people who consider their business to be ministry. The Bible does not exclude this possibility. If business is ministry, it is reasonable, as well as biblical, to anticipate that God would incline His ear to prayers for favor. Ministry requests are denominator issues and therefore fall within the realm of God's greater concern. Business that operates as a form of ministry is a noble undertaking, but we need to understand that it is dangerous territory.

> *And they came to Jerusalem. And He entered the temple and began to cast out the those who were buying and selling in the temple, and overturned the tables of the moneychangers and the seats of those who were selling doves... and He would not permit anyone to carry goods through the temple. And He*

> began to teach and say to them, "Is it not written, My house shall be called a house of prayer for all the nations? But you have made it a robbers den."
>
> **MARK 11:15–17**

Nowhere else in Scripture do we see Jesus outraged to this magnitude. Nowhere else do we see spiritual indignation so intense that it moves Him to such a physical response. I find that fact amazing when you consider the injustice He witnessed and the personal assaults He endured. How does this encounter in the temple even begin to compare with being spit upon? Why do the temple businessmen draw greater ire from Jesus than the Pharisees who plotted to kill Him? Over the entire course of a three-year-long controversial public ministry that ultimately led to His own cruel, torturous, undeserved death, this encounter in the temple marks the only recorded physical display of anger. (Some argue that it was not anger, but anyone who thinks the Lord is incapable of anger or wrath has spent little time in the Old Testament.) I have no doubt Jesus was angry. What provoked Him? I believe it was unfulfilled expectations.

That is precisely the reason I said operating a business as ministry is dangerous territory. Expectations are so much higher when you present your business as ministry. Never mind the expectations of the general public, even though they are in play.

Who among us has not been disappointed by a business that presented itself as a Christian enterprise? The truth of the matter is that the service, product, or transaction that disappointed us was probably no worse than what we would have received from any other business, but we expected something greater. The public expects something better from Christian enterprise, but I want to focus upon the Lord's expectations.

Ministry is a partnership with God. If He is not drawn in, it is not ministry at all. When you declare your business to be ministry, you need to understand that you have engaged in a partnership with God. You have committed yourself to a spiritual endeavor. It is a model for business that in most ways is contrary to the norm. Given the spiritual nature of the partnership, can business truly be conducted as ministry? Sure it can, and as such, God hears the prayers for blessing and greatly desires to place His favor upon the business.

If your business is your ministry, I am in complete agreement that it is wise, as well as biblical, to ask God to bless your business. It would be silly not to. It is a prayer for ministry, a request that no doubt delights the Lord. Just make certain that you understand what God expects from a ministry business in return for His favor. Many jump in only to discover it is not what they intended. Businesses that satisfy the requirement of a joint spiritual venture with God are rare. They are partnerships that cannot be entered into lightly. The Lord takes ministry very seriously, and with His favor come expectations.

Businessmen operating under the premise of ministry while neglecting godly expectation place their enterprise in danger. I believe that's what happened in the temple.

> *And they came to Jerusalem. And He entered the temple and began to cast out the those who were buying and selling in the temple, and overturned the tables of the moneychangers and the seats of those who were selling doves.*
> **MARK 11:15**

The businesses that ignited Jesus' spiritual indignation were located inside the temple. These were not ordinary establishments engaged in commerce on the streets of Jerusalem. These businesses were different—and not only in location but also in the nature of the businesses and the currency they were dealing in. These establishments were unique. Their supposed intent was to help facilitate temple worship. The proprietors were selling sacrificial animals to those who were coming to the temple for spiritual cleansing. Some were there to exchange spiritually unacceptable Roman currency for Jewish coins. From external appearances, these businesses were operating for the purpose of ministry. Why then would Jesus be so opposed to their operation? The answer is found at the end of verse 17.

> *"But you have made it a robber's den."*
> **MARK 15:17**

The businesses in the temple were cheating the customers. Exorbitant prices, tainted animals, and deliberate overcharges on currency exchange rates had become the normal business practices. The proprietors were able to leverage their unethical dealings against the spiritual needs and religious requirements of their customers. People needed these services to worship in the temple. What was supposed to serve as ministry business was no different from the commerce that was being conducted outside of ministry. The problem is that expectations are much higher, and more closely guarded by God, when business is conducted under the premise of ministry. Jesus's words and physical actions were justified based upon the expectations of the godly partnership.

There are a couple things that are important to note in this Scripture. The first is this: there were no civil ramifications of Jesus's action. He tore some stuff up and no doubt made some folks mad. Yet, we see no indication that it drew the attention of Roman authorities.

These businesses were evidently operating outside the jurisdiction of Roman law. In the eyes of the government, these businesses must have been Jewish ministry. If Jesus had violated Roman law, the Jewish leaders who wanted so badly to have Jesus put away would have brought civil accusations against Him. After He had overturned tables, cast people out, and accused them of being thieves, Scripture tells us that the priests and scribes were trying to find a way to destroy Him.

And the chief priests and the scribes heard this, and began seeking how to destroy Him.

MARK 15:18

If Jesus had violated Roman law, the priests and scribes would have had no need to seek a way to destroy Him; they could have easily gotten Him arrested. But civil law had not been broken because these businesses were operating as ministry. Jesus simply dissolved some underperforming ministry partnerships.

The second thing to note is that there was no outcry from those attending the temple. More importantly, there was no resistance from the accused proprietors. The cold, hard truth was that everyone there knew that Jesus's words were true. He was not making unfounded accusations. The temple businessmen were guilty of everything Jesus confronted them with. I imagine their only complaint would have been that Jesus walked past businesses every bit as unethical as theirs while on His way to the temple. What they may not have understood is that the consequences of conducting unfair business inside the gates of the temple were much more severe.

The same is true today. Conducting business inside the gates of ministry has its own set of requirements. When we come to the Lord in prayer and ask His favor upon our business, underwritten with the intent that it be considered our ministry, we must be careful. It is a business proposal that God refuses to take lightly. It comes with greater expectation and more severe consequences. When we truly understand all that it entails, this partnership is one that most will back away from. When we honestly examine our motives and our goals for business, most of us are more inclined to want to conduct business outside the temple. The exceptions are rare.

I am not suggesting that most people want to conduct unethical or unfair business. Nor am I suggesting that unethical business practices are acceptable in God's eyes so long as we don't operate under the guise of ministry. That is ridiculous. What I am suggesting is that business conducted under the premise of ministry is business that draws God's fullest attention, as well as His most intense response. The encounter in the temple makes that evident.

Like most other areas of spiritual life, when God's requirements differ from our own desires, we tend to create a compromise more suitable to our liking. In the case of business, we do not want the full-blown obligations of ministry, but we also don't want to miss the blessings, so we have settled somewhere in between. We have created businesstry.

Businesstry is a hybrid that seeks God's favor while applying a lighter, more business-friendly version of ministry. We may like it, but God is not impressed. Businesstry is lukewarm.

> *I know your deeds, that you are neither cold nor hot; I wish that you were cold or hot. So because you are lukewarm, and neither hot nor cold, I will spit you out of My mouth.*
>
> **REVELATION 3:15–16**

God only desires to hear and respond to our prayers for business if our business is indeed ministry, a partnership with Him in a spiritual endeavor. If that defines how your business operates, then I would emphatically encourage you to seek God's blessings and favor. He is anxious to respond, delighted to oblige. However, if you are engaged in businesstry, He only desires to spit your enterprise out of His mouth. It is dangerous territory.

How can you know that your business is truly ministry and not businesstry? We commonly consider a multitude of godly behaviors to be characteristic of a believer in Christ. These same characteristics would be evident in the life of a business, but don't be deceived. Attempting to apply Christian principles to the operation of your business does not qualify it as ministry. That behavior is the minimum expectation of belief in Christ. It is basic. It is fundamental.

The principles of Christianity are intended by God to be woven into the fabric of every aspect of our life. To include them in your business life is not any more noteworthy than applying them at home or at the grocery store or anywhere else. It is supposed to be who you are. In later chapters we will explore the application of these Christian principles in business. For now, we just need to acknowledge that although they must be present, those principles are not the single identifying element of business ministry. Christian principles are the starting line, not the finish line. Ministry is much more than business conducted ethically.

What else is required?

When the apostle Paul wrote letters to both Timothy and Titus, he made special effort to point out the requirements for ministers. Positions of ministerial leadership have their own special set of qualifications. Paul's instruction touched upon several different areas of conduct, but the general theme across all of them was the same: be above reproach. Conduct above reproach is the godly expectation for ministry. That is exactly the responsibility we assume when we present our business to God as ministry.

Beyond reproach does not mean that you are operating more ethically than some, or even most, of your business peers. It means that your practices are God-worthy. It is the only standard that ministry should be measured by. Are you ready to submit your business to that level of divine scrutiny?

Remember: what He will walk past in the street, He will not tolerate inside the temple. Are you prepared to do business inside the temple? Transactions, practices, alliances, words, and even motives are surrendered to the will of your partner in the spiritual endeavor. That is business ministry.

I like to believe that we are operating our own family business with Christian principles, but I am confident that we are not satisfying the requirements of ministry. I am only deceiving myself if I attempt to leverage God's blessing on our business with claims of ministry. He knows better. I cannot pray for God to bless what I know to be an earthly treasure, even if it is being operated ethically.

Another defining characteristic of ministry is a willingness to yield, a willingness to be led in whatever direction God chooses. That is not easy. As business owners, we like the feel of the steering wheel in our hands. We like to map out the direction. We want to set the course. We don't like to relinquish control. More often than not, my prayers end up being a request for God to bless the direction I have chosen.

"Lord, I know what needs to be done. I can steer. I just need You to fill the tank."

That is not good ministry. It is not even good Christianity, but it is a common mindset. We don't really want help in the wheelhouse, just the engine room. A business that claims to be ministry will constantly seek God's direction and is in continual surrender to His response.

My attempts have been spotty at best, well-intentioned but short-lived. It is a management style that would be much easier for me to maintain if it weren't for the fact that God's desire does not always make good business sense. Those are the times when we prefer to close our ears, grab the wheel, and do businesstry. It is then that ministry turns lukewarm, and our business partner, God, loses interest. If we are lucky, He just ignores the prayers for favor. If we are not so lucky, our table gets overturned. From a business perspective, it can happen at the unlikeliest of times.

Christians commonly attribute prospering in business to God's blessings. We link the degree of God's pleasure to financial success. If we are doing well, God is showing us favor.

That is not always the case, and it is never the case when we choose to move in our own direction. No doubt the vendors in the temple were doing well financially. But never do we read in Scripture where financial success in business delights God more than surrender and obedience.

God will allow us to move in a direction other than His, and it is possible that we can prosper. However, when we do, we step out from under the umbrella of His willingness to respond. It will not diminish His love and concern for you, just His concern over the endeavor. Obedience trumps good business. Obedience will usually require us to make decisions that do not make good business sense.

Now it happened that while the crowd was pressing around Him and listening to the word of God, He was

> *standing by the lake of Gennesaret; and He saw two boats lying at the edge of the lake; but the fishermen had gotten out of them and were washing their nets. And He got into one of the boats, which was Simon's, and asked him to put out a little way from the land. And He sat down and began teaching the people from the boat.*
>
> LUKE 5:1–3

Let's stop right there for just a moment. Jesus was teaching along the lakeshore. His words had attracted a large enough throng that He was being pressed by the crowd around Him. Simon—whom we know as Peter, a fisherman, a local businessman—was on the shore with his crew cleaning their nets after a night of fishing. I imagine from their close proximity and the amount of attention Jesus had drawn that Peter was able to hear what Jesus was teaching. This assumption is supported by Peter's willingness to allow Jesus to use his boat. Something that was said, perhaps coupled with some previous knowledge of the dynamic teacher, prompted Peter to do this favor for Jesus.

This favor is a bigger deal than it seems. The fishing boat is how Peter made his living; it is how he sustained himself. Essentially, the fisherman was letting Jesus borrow his business. Not only that, but Peter had already been up all night fishing, and now he was being asked to go out on the water again. Something in the words of Jesus resonated within the zealous, self-sufficient personality of Peter. He surrendered both his boat and his time to Jesus's request.

Peter and his crew pushed the boat back out into Lake Gennesaret. While together with Jesus in the boat, Peter was able to focus his full attention upon Him. He heard His words and saw His face. I am confident that everything Jesus did and said while in that vessel was spoken to the throng but directed at Peter. If you think I am taking undue liberty and reading too much into the significance Jesus placed upon teaching Peter, consider for a moment His intent for the zealous fisherman. Simon Peter was the rock that Jesus declared He would build His church upon.

> *I also say to you that you are Peter, and upon this rock I will build My church; and the gates of Hades will not overpower it.*
> **MATTHEW 16:18**

It is not out of the question to believe that this encounter was a profound teaching moment in the preparation of Peter. Based upon what happened next, Jesus's words made an impact.

> *When He had finished speaking, He said to Simon, "Put out into the deep water and let down your nets for a catch."*
> **LUKE 5:4**

Fishing was Peter's business, and he was quite accomplished. His crew had just toiled the entire night. Peter had spent the night applying all the knowledge and experience he had acquired over years of successful business, yet on this particular morning they had nothing to show for it. After catching no fish, the crew was outside the boat, busy cleaning their equipment in preparation for the next night's fishing. It is one of those necessary but annoying tasks that is made more frustrating by the lack of success. I've been there, and I'll bet you have too. Tired and frustrated after a long, difficult, unsuccessful day, you are then faced with all the mundane and tedious tasks that come with the job.

Now imagine that someone totally unfamiliar with your business, someone with no experience in your field comes along and suggests how to improve business. That was the situation with Peter and Jesus. Jesus, the son of a carpenter, tells the experienced fisherman what will need to be done to catch fish. The crew has fished all night, the nets have been cleaned, and now Jesus tells them to go out into the deep water and drop their nets again. From Peter's perspective this had to make absolutely no sense at all. He had spent the night fishing in the best spots, at the best time, and caught nothing. Dropping the nets in deep water that morning had all the marks of bad business.

But Peter did it anyway. That is why I believe the words Jesus spoke while in the boat had a profound impact upon Peter.

> *Simon answered and said, "Master, we worked hard all night and caught nothing, but I will do as You say and let down the nets."*
> **LUKE 5:5**

Peter surrendered the decision-making power of his business into the hands of Jesus. He obeyed the voice of God and made a business decision that made no sense. Peter's business was doing ministry. The result was astounding.

> *When they had done this, they enclosed a great quantity of fish, and their nets began to break; so they signaled to their partners in the other boat, for them to come and help them. And they came and filled both of the boats, so that they began to sink.*
> **LUKE 5:6–7**

What made no business sense at all turned into an incredibly good decision. The miraculous catch, which was nothing less than an outpouring of God's favor, was not given for the sake of expanding Peter's business. That was just a collateral reward. The miraculous catch was given to make a spiritual statement to all those who witnessed it, as well as all those who would hear about it. When business is serving as ministry and we surrender control of the business direction into the hands of our ministry partner, incredible spiritual events will occur. We may prosper as a result, but our prosperity is not the motive.

We can discover two simple litmus tests for business ministry in this Scripture:

1. If every decision made throughout the course of the year (or even the day) is based solely upon what makes the best business sense, it is a definite indication that you are not doing ministry.

2. If you are not seeing incredible spiritual events occurring in and around your business, it is another indication that you are not doing ministry.

I have already shared my belief that the morning Jesus spent on Lake Gennesaret was meant to be more than just teaching the masses and performing a public miracle. The encounter was intended to specifically target Peter. It worked.

> *But when Simon Peter saw that, he fell down at Jesus' feet, saying, "Go away from me, Lord, for I am a sinful man!" For amazement had seized him and all his companions because of the catch of fish which they had taken;*
>
> **LUKE 5:8–9**

Business ministry is unmistakable. It is also very rare. Scripture requires that as believers we must conduct business in an ethical, Christ-like manner, but it does not require that our business be ministry. Ministry is a choice we make. It is an agreement that we enter into with God, partners in a spiritual endeavor. And only when we enter into this ministry agreement does our business move from earthly treasure to heavenly treasure. As heavenly treasure, it places itself in a position of receiving God's favor and blessings. It is a partnership with expectations well beyond a normal Christian business, but the rewards are commensurate.

I think it is important to emphasize again that just like a personal surrender to Christian ministry, business ministry is a calling. It is not a scriptural requirement that your business serve as ministry. Ministry is a response of choice, much the same as Peter's. It does not happen without the beckoning of the Lord. It does not happen without yielding control, and it does not operate without producing visible spiritual results. It is rare. Before you petition God's blessing upon your business under the premise of ministry, make certain that it is a partnership that you sincerely desire. Then be prepared for what may happen next.

> *And so also were James and John, sons of Zebedee, who were partners with Simon. And Jesus said to Simon, "Do not fear, from now on you will be catching men." When they had brought their boats to land, they left everything and followed Him.*
>
> **LUKE 5:10–11**

They left everything and followed Him. These fishermen walked away from their business after what must have been the most significant and prosperous catch of their life. Equally amazing is that they walked away without even cashing in on the big catch. Profits, assets, and business future were left on the shore. They walked away. Are you really prepared to do business ministry?

I truly believe that Peter's experience on Lake Gennesaret is a template for the natural progression for those rare businesses that genuinely serve as ministry. In Peter's case, it all happened in a single morning, but typically the progression takes years, maybe even decades. The time frame is not as important as the template. By retracing the events of Peter's big morning on Lake Gennesaret, we can establish the elements of progression and read the template.

Here is how it goes: The words and teachings of Jesus arouse an interest within the business owner. It may begin as nothing more than a curiosity, as it did on the shoreline where Jesus was pressed. At some point curiosity leads to conviction, and casual interest grows into something more personal, more binding, as it did once Peter and Jesus were in the boat together. It is what James referred to as drawing near.

> *Draw near to God and He will draw near to you.*
> **JAMES 4:8**

In reality, it is not really a case of God drawing near to us. It is an enlightening, an awareness that He is near. We begin to feel for Him what He already feels for us. Peter drew near to God and was able to feel God near to him. Peter was now a businessman who had a relationship with God.

Peter's boat (his business) then became a platform for God to minister from: a useful tool for the kingdom's sake. This is the next step in the natural progression toward business ministry. Though

Peter was not actively involved in ministry, he was facilitating ministry. He was now a businessman who had a relationship with God and supported Kingdom ministry. Many fine businesses in America are providing boats for Jesus to teach and preach from. They are not ministries, but they facilitate ministry.

Sitting in the boat, with his eyes and ears upon the Lord, Peter listened and yielded to Jesus's ministry. As he did, his own knowledge and faith deepened. The result was a heart willing to follow the directions given by the Lord. This is where things become more difficult for business owners.

At times, God's directions may appear to make little sense, perhaps even as ridiculous as rowing out into the deep water and dropping the nets after a long night of catching nothing. If, like Peter, the business owner responds in faith, business becomes a spiritual endeavor. The business becomes an active instrument for the advancement of the gospel, and events that cannot be explained in terms of normal business operation begin to occur. The business's spiritual tracks are clearly seen in the commercial landscape. God's blessing pours out, His hand moves, and nets break from the amazing catch. Business and ministry become one.

In Peter's case, there was one final step in the progression. It is worth noting. Peter left everything and followed Jesus. When business is conducted as ministry, business owners are continually being transformed into a greater likeness of their Creator. They begin to view the human fraction from a godly perspective. Their interest shifts to the denominator. Focus turns to heavenly treasure, and business loses its luster. If we are ever able to reach that point, walking away like Peter is not difficult. All that is required is one simple request: follow Me. Business ministry is indeed rare, but it must be sheer delight in the eyes of God.

Does that sound like where you see yourself in business? If not, don't be upset. Do not spiritually beat yourself up if you are operating a Christian business that is not ministry. It is okay. Business ministry is not a biblical requirement. It is a response to a calling, and the Lord does not extend that call to everyone. Peter was not the only fisherman on the shoreline.

We err when we think that because we are Christians our business must serve as a ministry. Keep in mind that very few people are truly doing business ministry, and given how seriously God takes ministry, it would not be wise to try and fake it. We enter dangerous territory if we misrepresent business as ministry in our prayers with the hope of blessings in return. There has to be a better way to pray for our business.

CHAPTER 6

A BETTER WAY

My family and I are attempting to conduct business in a Christ-like manner, but our business is clearly not ministry. I understand that we are operating outside the temple gates. The business is without question an earthly treasure. At some point it will be separated from me, or I from it. I do not expect to see it in the heavenly realm. It will be left to moths and rust. As an earthly treasure, it is a numerator — or financial — concern. Though significant to me, based upon my understanding of Scripture, our business is of little importance to God. I get that. His focus is equipping me to properly deal with it. I matter to Him, and the way I conduct myself while doing business is where God's great concern lies. Jesus may have walked past the businesses outside the temple, but He died for the owners of those businesses. His connection to business is His love for those who work within it.

I no longer pray for God to bless our business, but I do pray constantly for Him to bless me, as well as those that I am in business with. I don't mean to bless us with sales or revenue. I mean bless my denominator. My prayer is that God will strengthen the qualities within me that should define me as being one of His while I am at my desk.

I pray that He will create in me the kind of person who treats others the way I desire to be treated when I am interacting with associates and customers. Help me to forgive those who trespass against me. Develop me, mold me, teach me, and yes, even chastise me if required. Do in me whatever is necessary for me to be more pleasing to you in my business life. Those are the things that Scripture tells us God desires to bless us with. That is the favor He so wants to grant.

Don't be misled. I struggle constantly with every one of the things that I ask for in prayer. I have conquered none of them. Just like Peter, most of the time I am forced to cry out in my heart, "Go away from me, Lord, for I am a sinful man!" Sometimes the days seem to be nothing more than a string of failure and spiritual disappointment. I open my mouth, and what I hate most about me pours out. I entertain motives that share nothing in common with God's desires. Days and weeks pass by with my heart and eyes focused like a laser beam on the numerator. I am guilty of wringing my hands over how to build a larger rust pile, creating blueprints for bigger barns in my mind, with little attention given to whether or not I am a reflection of the One who created me in His own image.

I am not above reproach. I may not even stack up well to my peers, let alone godly expectations. That should be my prayer concern for business. How can I ask God to bless my business when as a proprietor I am in such constant need of help? For me to be a reflection of Christ while doing business should be the favor that I seek. That is a business prayer that God hears. That is a business prayer that God cares about. That is a business prayer that satisfies the scriptural context of 1 Peter 5:7.

Casting all your anxiety on Him, because He cares for you.
1 PETER 5:7

Even beyond all the spiritual or moral qualities I hope to possess in business, I could stay busy just praying over the physical needs: prayers for physical strength and the stamina to persevere through trying times, prayers for diligence and clarity of mind when faced with difficult decisions, prayers for the continued good health that makes it possible to be at work. Prayers of intercession for the health and safety of those who work with us will help to keep me mindful of their needs. Prayers of praise and thanksgiving will create a heart of gratitude that is able to quench an anxious fire. Were I faithful enough to do it, I could spend an hour in business prayer each day and never mention anything financial. There is no shortage of things that a Christian businessperson should pray for, but they have much more to do with the person than the business.

Years ago, when we were first starting out in business, I was already leaning toward the opinion that the mechanics of business had little relevance to God's kingdom. I was also confident from years of study that people were of utmost importance to God. His greater concern was for me, as well as the people with whom I would be doing business. My business life could not be disconnected from my spiritual obligations and desires. Any endeavor that separates me from God for any length of time cannot possibly be within His will. To succeed at business and fail in my relationship with the Lord would be a grave mistake. On the other hand, I knew that I had been created in the likeness of God, able to think, to reason, to prepare, to learn, and to apply. To not make the best possible use of those gifts would be an incredible waste and disappointment to the Giver of the gifts. There had to be a way to satisfy both biblical truths. I was confident that God would not move me in a direction that conflicted with biblical truth.

CHAPTER 7

WHATEVER

A common practice in business today is to develop a mission statement. The mission statement is exactly what the name implies: a declaration of what a business or corporation feels is its purpose. It is a brief explanation as to why the business exists, and what it intends to do. Overall, I agree with the idea. Everyone working within an organization should have some understanding of the intended purpose of their labor.

The length of these statements can vary from a single sentence to a long list of bullet points, but a few catchwords have become almost mandatory within every company's mission statement. You will almost always see the following words: safety, service, quality, and environment. Their order varies, but they all appear somewhere within the statement. These are all excellent goals for business, but the honest truth is that if they stand in the way of greater profitability, they will become secondary.

I have to grin when I see these corporate statements framed and hanging in the reception areas of the businesses I visit. Nobody seems to be honest enough to list larger profits as part of their mission.

Profit is the ultimate goal of business, and all the catchwords that are used in mission statements are the makeup that put a more attractive and appealing appearance on what may otherwise be seen as corporate greed. Shareholders are interested in dividends. Lenders are interested in revenue. Imagine trying to renew a business loan at the bank with the explanation that even though you failed to generate a profit, you did manage to hit all your mission statement goals. You will leave empty-handed.

I agree with the idea of mission statements. I even agree with the popular buzzwords. Companies should be environmentally responsible. They should supply a safe workplace and be community conscious, but the cold, hard truth in business is that none of it matters if you don't make a profit. The problem is that profiting in business has developed some negative connotations in our society. Successful businesses in America, especially the larger ones, are often perceived as selfish and greedy. Though it may be true of some, it is not true of most. To remain healthy, a business must prosper, it must generate a profit. My hope for our own business, as well as the businesses of other believers, is that we will prosper. Is it possible to prosper in business and still continue to please God?

Prosperity is one of those biblical topics that can be confounding. As a result, you find conflicting opinions regarding its application in Christian life. There are those who have established successful ministries based upon the belief that prosperity is there for the asking. They teach that God desires to pour His riches out upon you. Just stake your claim. On the other hand, there are entire sects of Christianity that were founded on the principle of a minimalist lifestyle. The Bible seems to support both viewpoints. You can even find both within the same book.

> *Let them shout for joy and rejoice, who favor my vindication; And let them say continually, "The Lord be magnified, Who delights in the prosperity of His servant."*
>
> **PSALM 35:27**

> *The wicked, in the haughtiness of his countenance, does not seek Him. All his thoughts are, "There is no God." His ways prosper at all times. Your judgments are on high, out of his sight.*
>
> **PSALM 10:4–5**

Is prosperity the mark of a servant who delights the Lord, or is it the mark of a wicked man who denies that there is a God?

The answer is, of course, both. Prosperity is not a measuring stick for breadth of faith or depth of wickedness. Everyone, from the most wicked all the way up the scale to the most faithful, has the potential to prosper. As I stated earlier, we possess by virtue of our divinely inspired design, the capacity to provide for our physical needs. We have the ability to generate income as well as profit regardless of our belief in God. Psalm 10:4–5 makes it clear that those who do not even believe that there is a God can prosper. Not just prosper, but prosper at all times. That would seem to indicate that prosperity has no connection with godliness. Yet, Psalm 35:27 declares that the prosperity of a believer has the potential to delight God. It is easy to see why so many people within Christianity get conflicted.

There is no need for confusion or uncertainty on this topic. Scripture does not contradict itself regarding prosperity. In fact, the Bible is quite clear when you examine it more closely. Wealth, riches, and profit are available to everyone, believer or not. I don't think there is any need to explain how nonbelievers can amass wealth. We have witnessed it in every generation, and it is not automatically the product of wickedness or questionable business practices. Many people who are not Christians but possess many fine qualities prosper in business. Some have done it with sheer genius, some with a monumental work ethic, and others with crazy good luck. None have done it by God's favor if they have no relationship with Him. They have prospered by their own plan, and God has allowed them freedom to do it.

But there is another form of prosperity, which is biblical, and the Lord's delight is reserved for those who prosper according to His plan.

> *The Lord was with **Joseph**, so he became a successful man. And he was in the house of his master, the Egyptian. Now the master saw that the Lord was with him and how the Lord caused all that he did to prosper in his hand.*
>
> **GENESIS 39:2–3**

> *God said to **Solomon**, "Because you had this in mind, and did not ask for riches, wealth or honor, or the life of those who hate you, nor have you even asked for long life, but you asked for yourself wisdom and knowledge, that you may rule My people over whom I have made you king, wisdom and knowledge have been granted to you. And I will give you riches and wealth and honor, such as none of the kings who were before you has possessed nor those who will come after you."*
>
> **2 CHRONICLES 1:11–12**

> *He [**Uzziah**] did right in the sight of the Lord according to all that his father Amaziah had done. He continued to seek God in the days of Zechariah, who*

had understanding through the vision of God; and as long as he sought the Lord, God prospered him.

2 CHRONICLES 26:4–5

There are some common threads in these examples. Each of these three men chose to seek God, and in response to that desire, God chose to prosper them. This is the biblical formula. It is God's unique plan for prosperity of a servant. Just like the three listed examples, we too are candidates for prosperity. Unlike the prosperity of unbelievers, ours is a prosperity that delights the Lord. Prosperity, therefore, cannot possibly be inherently evil.

Don't allow yourself to get tangled up in the misconceptions of those who would begrudge success. Don't toil physically, only to wrangle spiritually with whether or not Christians are allowed to become wealthy in business. Profit is biblically acceptable. Have you forgotten the size of the catch that God used to reward Peter's obedience?

When they had done this, they enclosed a great quantity of fish, and their nets began to break.

LUKE 5:6

That is a very profitable catch, a catch that the other fishermen along the shore could not match. Was it the product of selfish greed? Of course not. Peter's incredible catch was the product of obedience to the instructions of the Lord. Prosperity is not considered by God to be evil if it is preceded by obedience.

Pray for the peace of Jerusalem:
"May they prosper who love you."

PSALM 122:6

> *Beloved, I pray that in all respects you may prosper and be in good health, just as your soul prospers.*
>
> 3 JOHN 1:2

Notice the clear distinction made in 3 John 1:2. John was asking God for prosperity in "all" respects. He prayed for physical prosperity to match their spiritual prosperity. Physical prosperity, including wealth, possessions, and power were granted by God throughout Scripture as a reward for obedience. Joseph, Solomon, and Uzziah, as well as the many others you can find in the Scriptures, shared the common thread of obedience, and God chose to reward them with prosperity.

The second thread they shared was as critical as the first. They shared a common motive. Prosperity was the consequence, not the pursuit. Obedience did not have prosperity as its motive. It is here, at the motive, where I believe many individuals and entire ministries jump off the tracks. Any one of the three men—Joseph, Solomon, Uzziah—would have gladly forfeited wealth to maintain their relationship with God. The prosperity they enjoyed could not equal their treasure in the Lord.

So much of what is being taught and practiced in Christian business today is exactly reversed. Prosperity is the spiritual motive. We act in obedience with the hope, or even the expectation that it will bring us prosperity. How disappointing that must be in the eyes of God. Obedience has no divine value if it is done for any other reason than to please God. Solomon did not have an eye on riches when he chose wisdom as the attribute he most desired. His sincere desire was to lead the people with godly wisdom. The ability to make decisions that served people and pleased God was more important to

Solomon than his own safety and well-being. Joseph did not request that God allow him to become wealthy in the court of the Egyptian master. Peter did not ask for an incredible catch of fish. All of them acted out of pure obedience. That is the type of motive that delights God, the kind that He chooses to prosper.

In business, acting from a pure and unselfish motive is not easily done. It is a continuous battle, even for those who desire to pursue righteousness. Personal matters such as motive can be difficult to judge. Outward appearance does not always indicate what lies beneath. People can be fooled, but God is not deceived. He knows very well our decision-making process. He sees our units of measure. Fortunately, God also understands that righteousness in our motives is a journey. He recognizes the battle we face. He knows perfecting our motives is an ongoing process.

A chasm of difference still lies between my own self-serving motives and the example of Peter. When I consider again what occurred that morning on the shore of Lake Gennesaret, I clearly see how far I have yet to go in my journey toward righteous motives. Peter had just experienced a remarkable catch. From a business standpoint, it had been a very good morning for him. Over the years, our business has posted some above-average growth. We have had some good days, but we've never had a day that would equal what happened to Peter that morning. I get excited on our good days, inspired to push the business to a new level. I want to drill deeper and seek new ways to sustain the growth. The very last thing I want to do as the business shows signs of success is to walk away, but that is exactly what Peter did. He walked away, leaving perhaps the biggest catch of his career tangled up in the nets.

Could you walk away? Would you be willing to leave a profitable business behind in response to God's "follow me"? Would you trade your business for obedience, no questions asked? Could you leave profits lying on the ground? I cannot claim that level of obedience. Peter's decision was one that I am not yet capable of making. I could claim that Peter acted in response to a face-to-face request, and if I were to somehow find myself in that same situation, I would probably respond as he did. You may be fooled. I may even fool myself, but God is not deceived. The truth is that I don't know for certain if I would or not. I still have work to do regarding motive if it is my desire for God to truly delight in my prosperity.

Work ethic is the third thing that we should note about the people in Scripture who God chose to prosper. God prospered them in the midst of their own efforts. None sat idle waiting expectantly upon the Lord's provision. Joseph continued to serve faithfully in the court of his master. Solomon continued to serve and lead the people of Israel. Peter cast out into the deep water and let down the nets. He kept on fishing. Jesus's ability to provide the miraculous catch was not dependent upon Peter's physical effort. It could have been done without him, but Jesus chose to provide the great catch in response to Peter's obedient effort.

To prosper biblically requires that you apply yourself to the task. Not because God needs your labor, but because He needs to see your willingness to labor. We need to be engaged, to continue in the effective use of all the tools we have been given. I don't believe God is going to participate in a slothful prosperity.

As Christian businesspeople, we need not wrestle with the notion that profit is evil. Prosperity is not merely allowed, according to Scripture, but it can be a spiritual delight. If the single greatest desire of our heart is to seek God, and our motives are pure—if we remain steadfast in our obedience and our work ethic—then the financial success we enjoy will delight the Lord.

I want to succeed in business. I want to prosper. I emphatically oppose the supposition in our culture that profit is evil. I am convinced that profit and prosperity fit within the framework of Christianity. As I considered writing a mission statement for our business, it was critical for me to construct it around the two things that I knew to be true:

1. My relationship with the Lord must not be compromised due to our business.

2. Our business must profit to survive.

I was certain that within Scripture were ample texts that provided instruction for the operation of a financially prosperous, godly business. If the prosperity of His servants delights the Lord, then it is reasonable to believe He would provide instructions on how it is to be done. I began with the basics: the greatest commandments.

In business, as in every other area of life, as Christians we are expected to fulfill the two greatest commandments.

> *"Teacher, which is the great commandment in the Law?" And He said to him, "'You shall love the Lord your God with all your heart, and with all your soul, and with all your mind.' This is the great and foremost commandment. The second is like it, 'You shall love your neighbor as yourself.' On these two commandments depend the whole Law and the Prophets."*
> **MATTHEW 22:36–40**

Business life is not exempt from these instructions. They are called great and foremost for good reason. These commandments are intended by God to be the fundamental basis for our behavior regardless of where we are or whom we are with. Too often the feeling, even among Christians, is that business operates under its own set of rules; spiritual guidelines do not apply. Not so. Christian business must fulfill the two great commandments. I absolutely believe it can be accomplished. Not only can it be accomplished, but it can be done while realizing a profit.

Satisfying the two great commandments while generating a fair and honest profit was my goal in business. I wanted a mission statement that conveyed this objective. Paul's letter to the Philippians is where I found exactly what I hoped to be our mission in business.

MISSION STATEMENT
Whatever is true.
Whatever is honorable.
Whatever is right.
Whatever is pure.
Whatever is lovely.
Whatever is of good repute.
If there is any excellence, and anything worthy of praise,
Let your mind dwell on these things.

PHILIPPIANS 4:8

CHAPTER 8

VOICES

I will admit that on the surface, the chosen mission statement is not dynamic. It is not an attention grabber. There is no wow factor. It almost reads more like a scout pledge than the mission of a corporation. However, if you spend a little time below the surface, you will catch a glimpse of its power. If you spend time trying to engineer its application, you will appreciate the depth of its challenge. The "wow" is not in what it is able to accomplish within the business, but rather what it can accomplish within those who operate the business.

The intent is the exact opposite of the contemporary mindset. The prevailing philosophy is to construct a framework of noble corporate policy that can be used to create an environment that will develop employees into individuals of honor and good character. That seems entirely backward to me. It depicts business as the standard of excellence that the employees should pursue.

Employees should not reflect the excellence of a corporation. The corporation should reflect the excellence of its employees. Our mission statement focuses upon the people within the business. The values and ideals listed in that statement develop lives of character. When lives of character exercise the divine gifts of thought and reason, wisdom is gained. When a strong work ethic is applied to wisdom, prosperity is achieved. When prosperity is achieved through godly principles by His servants, God is delighted. That is the type of business I hope we can build. It all hinges upon the "whatever."

The thing about "whatever" is that it involves precisely what it says. In a field of "ever," we must be able to focus upon the "what." Being able to identify the correct "what" is the fundamental element of wisdom. When given the chance by God to choose whatever he would like for himself, Solomon made the perfect choice. Solomon sorted through the field of "ever" and chose wisdom as his "what."

> God said to Solomon, "Because you had this in mind, and did not ask for riches, wealth, or honor, or the life of those who hate you, nor have you even asked for long life, but you asked for yourself **wisdom** and knowledge, that you may rule My people, over whom I have made you king, wisdom and knowledge have been granted to you. And I will give you riches and wealth and honor, such as none of the kings who were before you has possessed nor those who will come after you."
> **2 CHRONICLES 1:11–12**

There were a lot of very appealing things out there for Solomon to choose from. He could have picked health, fame, riches, security, or anything else he desired. The number of possible options that would cross the average person's mind is staggering. I shudder to think which direction my own deliberations would have gone in that situation. How was Solomon able to arrive at the choice he made? More importantly, how can we make the correct choices when faced with difficult decisions? How can we keep our focus on building the individual first, when building the business is how most people will measure success?

It is all about the voices. I am convinced that the single most important element of good decision-making, whether in business or any other area of life, is the ability to discern the voices in your head.

Let's be honest: there is a lot of noise up there. You are hearing from customers, suppliers, bankers, and accountants. Everybody has a need, a want, or an opinion. Most of these needs involve the two most measured and rationed commodities: time and money. Add to that a whole slew of local, state, and federal agencies: IRS, EPA, DOT, FDA, ICC, DOL, and OSHA. There is no shortage of codes, regulations, laws, and requirements that add to the chatter in your brain. You hear the voices of those with needs outside of business: family, friends, church, and community. Admit it or not, your head also plays host to bands of demons vying for attention. Their sole purpose is to turn your focus inward. The demons are hard to ignore, especially in the difficult times, because they pitch self-pleasure.

Yes, there is a lot of noise up there. If you operate or manage a business, a multitude of voices occupy your mind. Somewhere among all of them is the voice of God.

> *I will instruct you and teach you in the way which you should go; I will counsel you with my eye upon you.*
> **PSALM 32:8**

Rest assured: if you believe in the Lord Jesus, His voice is somewhere among the chorus in your head. It is there for counsel, for guidance, for direction and instruction. I used to think that God's guidance was of the general type. I did not consider His instruction to be specific in nature. It only served as a "do good, not evil" backdrop to the overall deliberations going on in my mind. I have since learned that I was wrong.

> *And your ears will hear a word behind you, "This is the way, walk in it," whenever you turn to the right or to the left.*
>
> **ISAIAH 30:21**

The instructions given by God can be quite specific. We see examples throughout Scripture. When Noah was instructed to build the ark, he was not only given the specific dimensions, he was told what kind of wood to use and where to place the door and the window. God's instructions for Joshua's conquest of Jericho were also specific. When carried out according to the Lord's detailed instructions, the plan worked to perfection.

When we read these accounts in Scripture, we tend to make the totally unfounded assumption that God's voice was the only one in their ear. This assumption is unreasonable, especially in light of the major undertakings they involved. The many people involved were no doubt offering opinions and alternate plans. Add to all of these the voice of reason and that of the host of demons determined to foil God's plan.

Men like Abraham, Noah, Moses, Joshua, and Daniel do not get the credit they deserve if we assume that the lone voice in their heads was God's. Like us, they had to discern that voice. From them, we learn that the Lord does not just work His will in terms of general precepts. He also deals in the details. God may be whispering the correct decision in our ear, but we miss it because He is being drowned out by all the other voices that we are more inclined to recognize. So many ideas, so many opinions, so much advice, and so many different directions bombard our minds. How can we be better able to discern the voice of God? How can we hear the instruction and choose the correct path?

> *Trust in the Lord with all your heart*
> *And do not lean on your own understanding.*
> *In all your ways acknowledge Him,*
> *And He will make your paths straight.*
>
> **PROVERBS 3:5–6**

In the third chapter of Proverbs, Solomon, the definitive mortal authority on wisdom, laid out the criteria for discerning godly direction. There are three requirements.

The first requirement is to "trust in the Lord with all your heart." There is a wonderful illustration of this in the Gospel of Matthew. It involved Peter. That alone would lead you to conclude it was memorable.

> *And in the fourth watch of the night He*
> *came to them, walking on the sea.*
> *When the disciples saw Him walking on the sea, they*
> *were terrified, and said, "It is a ghost!" And they*
> *cried out in fear. But immediately Jesus spoke to them,*
> *saying, "Take courage, it is I; do not be afraid."*
> *Peter said to Him, "Lord, if it is You, command*
> *me to come to You on the water."*
> *And He said, "Come!" And Peter got out of the boat,*
> *and walked on the water and came toward Jesus.*
>
> **MATTHEW 14:25–29**

It had been a big day for the disciples. They had just witnessed and participated in Jesus's miraculous feeding of the five thousand using five loaves of bread and two fishes. The men were no doubt tired, and the crowd still pressed around them. Jesus instructed his disciples to get into the boat and go to the other side of the lake. It was three o'clock in the morning, and they were several hundred yards offshore when Jesus approached the boat. He was walking atop the water to meet up with them.

Scripture says that His disciples did not recognize Him. They thought it was a ghost and cried out in fear. When Jesus spoke, Peter thought he identified His voice. However, Peter was not certain because he responded, "Lord *if* it is you, command me to come to You on the water."

Peter did not have hard physical evidence that what he was seeing out on the water was Jesus. He trusted that it was, and when the Lord spoke again, saying, "Come," Peter responded. He stepped over the side of the boat and walked on the water. Again, we assume that Jesus's voice was the only one in Peter's head, and again that is unreasonable. Based upon what was at stake, I don't think I am taking unfounded liberty to suggest that Peter had to hear God's voice through the chatter of multiple others. He was a fisherman. Years of knowledge and common sense had to be screaming, "Don't do it, you will drown!"

The disciples may have been reminding him, "Peter, what if it is not Him?"

The chorus of demons were likely asking, "What is to be gained?"

Through it all, the voice that Peter was able to identify and focus upon was that of Jesus. Peter heard "come" over everything else. We will not get to the point where we can clearly discern the voice of God until we are willing to "trust Him with all of our heart."

When we examine the second criteria outlined by Solomon, it is easy to see why trust is so critical. As we read, "And do not lean on your own understanding," we need to make particular note of the words *lean* and *own* in this verse. Understanding is a good thing. Scripture does not only encourage us, but it also instructs us to gain understanding. Throughout the Bible we see an emphasis upon understanding.

> *Is not wisdom found among the aged?*
> *Does not long life bring understanding?*
> **JOB 12:12**, NIV

> *Blessed are those who find wisdom,*
> *those who gain understanding.*
> **PROVERBS 3:13**, NIV

> *I run in the path of your commands,*
> *for you have broadened my understanding.*
> **PSALM 119:32**, NIV

> *My son, do not let wisdom and understanding out of*
> *your sight, preserve sound judgment and discretion.*
> **PROVERBS 3:21**, NIV

> *Get wisdom, get understanding;*
> *do not forget my words or turn away from them.*
> **PROVERBS 4:5**, NIV

Solomon did not suggest that we be void of understanding. He was exhorting us not to *lean* on our *own* understanding. To *lean* on it would mean that it props us up. If what we lean on gets taken away or fails, we fall. It is important for us to gain and apply understanding, but our *own* understanding by itself is not enough. We need to be propped up by something other than just our own understanding. We need to lean on something greater, something stronger, something more stable, something more secure.

> *The mind of man plans his way,*
> *But the Lord directs his steps.*
> **PROVERBS 16:9**

In this proverb of Solomon, we see the two working in tandem: human plans and the Lord's direction. Human understanding is applied and placed into action through God's specific instruction. It is so difficult for business types to stray from our own understanding. We depend upon it continually, and it usually serves us well. Most prefer to be propped up by our own understanding because it is what we trust. There is a danger in that. When our own understanding is all that props us up, we are no longer able to hear God's voice. It was certainly not Peter's own understanding that caused him to step over the side of the boat while he was hundreds of yards offshore. It was Peter's mind that devised the plan, but it was the Lord who directed the steps.

When our own understanding is the only voice we respond to, we are destined to fall. It is not because we are not good businesspeople or even that we are acting outside of God's will. We fall because the voice of God cannot be heard over the roar of our own understanding. The plans we devise may be good, but they have their greatest chance of success when God directs the steps.

Keep in mind that Peter initiated this miraculous endeavor. Jesus was on His way to the boat when the disciples saw Him. He was coming to them as they sat in fear. Jesus did not initially command Peter to step over the side and come to Him. Jesus would have been fine with Peter waiting in the boat with the other disciples. It was Peter's idea to get out. He asked Jesus to command him to walk upon the water. It was a good plan, well devised. Then he waited for the Lord's response. When Jesus said, "Come," Peter's step had been directed.

In the eyes of anyone else, this was a ridiculous idea. Not only did it defy the laws of nature, but it lacked common sense, and it was completely unnecessary. Peter was not a stupid man, nor was he ignorant of the consequence of failure. He was a fisherman. Understanding the danger of the sea was second nature to him. Why, then, would he even want to attempt to do something that pointed so clearly to failure? Did he want to prove to the other disciples that he could do something great? Was it so he could show off his faith? Was it just for a thrill? I don't think so.

I believe Peter's motive was sincere. Peter simply wanted to draw more intimately near to Jesus. With an incredible love for the Lord and a faith so real that he literally entrusted his own life upon Jesus's command, Peter desired an even greater connection. Walking on the water was not his motive. Drawing nearer to Jesus was his motive, and as a result, something that was otherwise impossible was accomplished.

Even though we may be knowledgeable, intelligent, hardworking people with a solid dose of common sense, our understanding is inadequate at times because it is based upon our own vision, our own thoughts, and our own interpretations. As our minds devise plans, we must listen. We must turn down the volume of our own understanding so we can hear the voice of God whispering in our ear whether to turn to the right or left. We must learn to prop ourselves up on a greater understanding than our own.

> *"For My thoughts are not your thoughts,*
> *Nor are your ways My ways," declares the Lord.*
> *"For as the heavens are higher than the earth,*
> *So are My ways higher than your ways*
> *And My thoughts than your thoughts.*
>
> **ISAIAH 55:8–9**

Unlike the example of Peter walking on water, oftentimes the higher thought, the greater understanding does not confirm our plans. We do not get the response we are looking for from God. The answer is not always, "Come!" Sometimes, while all the other voices say yes, the higher thought is no. The steps that the Lord directs may share little in common with the ones we have mapped out ourselves. The plan we have devised may get completely redrawn by the voice of God, redrawn in a manner that makes little sense. Of all the many examples of God's head-scratching plans in Scripture, my personal favorite is from the Old Testament book of Judges.

Gideon had assembled a formidable army to fight the Midianites. He had 32,000 men camped in the valley near the hill of Moreh. The Lord spoke to Gideon and told him that he had too many men.

> *The Lord said to Gideon, "The people who are with you are too many for Me to give Midian into their hands, for Israel would become boastful, saying, 'My own power has delivered me.' Now therefore come, proclaim in the hearing of the people, saying, 'Whoever is afraid and trembling, let him return and depart from Mount Gilead.'" So 22,000 people returned, but 10,000 remained. Then the Lord said to Gideon, "The people are still too many; bring*

them down to the water and I will test them for you there. Therefore it shall be that he of whom I say to you, 'This one shall go with you,' he shall go with you; but everyone of whom I say to you, 'This one shall not go with you,' he shall not go." So he brought the people down to the water. And the Lord said to Gideon, "You shall separate everyone who laps the water with his tongue as a dog laps, as well as everyone who kneels to drink." Now the number of those who lapped, putting their hand to their mouth, was 300 men; but all the rest of the people kneeled to drink water. The Lord said to Gideon, "I will deliver you with the 300 men who lapped and will give the Midianites into your hands; so let all the other people go, each man to his home."

JUDGES 7:2–7

Gideon and his three hundred water-lapping men defeated the Midianites. This theme of God's plan appearing not to make sense is carried out throughout Scripture. From Abraham, all the way to Jesus's death on the cross, I am amazed at how God's higher ways work. Who among us, if we had the authority to do so, would not have stopped the cruel execution of Jesus? Our own mortal understanding would have not permitted such an injustice to occur. But by so doing we would have cheated humanity out of redemption. It was a plan we could not have seen. It was a thought higher than our own. Clearly His thoughts are higher than my thoughts, and His ways are higher than my ways.

From a military standpoint, the net result of God's battle plan was that Gideon and his three hundred men defeated the Midianites, but the victory was secondary to how it was attained. God put something more significant than victory into play when He devised the battle plan. The remarkable part of this text, the powerful message conveyed is the discipline, not the victory. I would have made strong opposition to such a radical culling of the troops. God's voice would not have been heard in my head over the loud voice of reason. Maybe three hundred men would be enough, but why not take all 32,000 and be sure? Doing it my way would have also won the battle, but it would not have accomplished everything that the Lord desired. It would not have served God's greater purpose. My own understanding does not have the depth of His, so it may satisfy my need, but it leaves His work undone.

When I consider this principle from a business perspective, I have to wonder how many times I have ignored God's instruction while marching into battle 32,000 strong. I may have accomplished what I had set out to do, but I never even got close to fulfilling God's purpose. More rust, more moths, no eternal treasure, and very little glory for God. When I lean on my own understanding, it is difficult to hear the voice of God.

The third criteria outlined by Solomon in Proverbs 3 is "in all your ways acknowledge Him." There are a lot of "ways" in business. The way you think, the way you plan, the way you communicate, the way you treat associates, the way you treat customers, the way you make sales, the way you negotiate and fulfill contracts, the way you deal with adversity and fatigue, the way you handle success, the way you receive criticism, the way you dispense criticism, the way you discipline, the way you exhort, the way you forgive, and the list goes on. There are a lot of "ways," and Scripture admonishes us to "acknowledge Him" in all of them. Is that really possible?

Most people associate "acknowledge Him" only in terms of prayer, but Proverbs 3:6 instructs otherwise. Acknowledgment of God is intended to be a critical element of all our actions, a component of every behavior. So, what does it mean to acknowledge? *Webster's New World College Dictionary Fourth Edition*[2] lists the following among its definition:

1. To admit to be true, or as stated; confess

2. To recognize the authority or claims of

3. To express thanks

I believe the acknowledgment that Solomon is advocating combines all three of the definitions listed above. What we must do is take each one of the many "ways" in business and hold them up beside the definition of acknowledge. For instance, does the way I think while I am at work confess Scripture to be true? Does it recognize the authority of God's claims? Does it express thanks? What about the way I negotiate and fulfill contracts? Do I satisfy the definition of "acknowledge" with regard to all of my business dealings? Nothing is exempt when the instruction is "in all your ways."

Can you discern the voice of God? Are you able to recognize it? Can you identify it from among the many other voices in your head? The ability to do so is critical if it is your desire to do business in a manner pleasing to Him. It is unreasonable to think that His will be the only words, the only ideas, or the only plans that swirl about in our minds. So long as there are decisions to be made and problems to be solved, there will always be multiple directions that we must

---

2. "Acknowledge," Webster's New World College Dictionary Fourth Edition (Webster's New World, 1999).

choose from. If we follow the instruction of Solomon, we can learn to pick out the Lord's voice, and within that voice we find direction.

Trust in the Lord with all your heart
And do not lean on your own understanding.
In all your ways acknowledge Him,
and He will make your paths straight.

PROVERBS 3:5–6

CHAPTER 9

SHOWING UP IN THE VINEYARD

God may not care about business, but if we profess to be a follower of His, He cares how we conduct business. It should be the natural extension and the inevitable result of acknowledging Him in all our ways. The unfortunate truth is that many times we are more interested in professing than we are in conducting. We are all about including the familiar symbols of Christianity and Scripture verses on our business cards and letterhead. We incorporate them into our company names and logos. We create organizations, associations, directories, and alliances that are intended to differentiate us from other businesses. We get a sense of spiritual satisfaction from publicly declaring our connection to Christ. I am not opposed to all the physical marks, and I am not condemning the practice of publicly displaying them. How could I? It would be incredibly hypocritical given that our company mission statement is a passage from Philippians. The public profession of our beliefs is expected of us. The mouth does matter, but in Scripture, it rarely plays the starring role. It is the supporting cast for godly actions and a sincere heart.

> *For with the heart a person believes, resulting in righteousness, and with the mouth he confesses, resulting in salvation.*
>
> **ROMANS 10:10**

> *Let the words of my mouth and the meditation of my heart Be acceptable in your sight, O Lord, my rock and my Redeemer.*
>
> **PSALM 19:14**

Did you notice the disproportion in Psalm 19:14: words of the mouth versus meditation of the heart? Meditation of the heart is a constant condition, while words of the mouth are fleeting by comparison. Meditation of the heart is akin to acknowledging in all your ways, and without it, the words of our mouth are in vain.

> *This people honors Me with their lips,*
> *But their heart is far away from Me,*
> *But in vain do they worship Me.*
>
> **MATTHEW 15:8–9**

The confession of our mouth and the familiar physical symbols of our allegiance to Christ are only significant if they are not the lone connection to our spiritual claim. It reminds me of a quote by Margaret Thatcher, the former prime minister of Great Britain. She was speaking about power.

> *"Being a leader is like being a lady. If you have to remind people you are, you aren't."*
>
> **MARGARET THATCHER**[3]

---

3. "Margaret Thatcher Showed What True Leadership Is," Forbes, updated April 23, 2013, https://www.forbes.com/sites/forbesleadershipforum/2013/04/08/margaret-thatcher-showed-what-true-leadership-is/?sh=4fab8b4f7f84.

The same could be said of Christian business. If you have to tell people that you are a Christian business, you probably aren't. It should be evident without the declaration. Those working inside and outside the business should be able to identify you as a Christian businessperson without the physical marks. Your conduct will profess what you believe much more profoundly than your business card or letterhead will. God is not as concerned with who we say we are as He is with who we prove ourselves to be. He is not interested in what we say we will do, but rather what we actually do.

> *But what do you think? A man had two sons, and he came to the first and said, "Son go work today in the vineyard." And he answered, "I will not"; but afterward he regretted it and went. The man came to the second and said the same thing; and he answered, "I will, sir"; but he did not go.*
> **MATTHEW 21:28–30**

I will ask the same question that Jesus asked the chief priests and the elders of the church in the very next verse.

> *"Which of the two did the will of his father?"*
> **MATTHEW 21:31**

The obvious answer is the first son. What is often overlooked in this short parable is the way that it occurred. After answering no to his father's request, the first son regretted what he had done. That regret originated in his heart. The meditation of his heart was focused on his love for his father and his desire to be obedient. That meditation traveled to his mind and then manifested itself in his feet and his hands. At that point the son was useful to his father. Also at that point, any profession from his mouth regarding obedience became valid.

The profession of the second son's mouth was never substantiated by the meditation of his heart. Therefore, it proved to be of no use to the father, and the words of his mouth were an empty profession. What a tragic injustice we do to God if we profess an association with Christ that implies a manner of doing business that is consistent with biblical principles, while on the back side of that cross we conduct ourselves no differently than any other establishment. We say yes, but like the second son, we are a no-show when it comes to action.

Perhaps the reason so many people think God cares about business is the multitude of Scripture devoted to how we should conduct business. The Bible gives clear guidelines, specific practices, and expected behaviors for godly business. But like the parable of the two sons, these Scriptures target the businessperson rather than the business itself.

The vineyard in Jesus's parable was not what was important to the father. His sons were what mattered to him. The way they conducted themselves and their obedience to his request was the focus of the father's concern. The same is true for our business. Our Father is not intent upon creating a godly business. He wants to build up a godly businessperson.

All the biblical business principles originate within our souls, in the sincere spiritual heart. From there they travel to the mind and then spread themselves to the hands, the feet, and the mouth. The response of the hands and the steps of the feet serve to validate the words of the mouth. The three work in tandem to create a profession of faith that is real. Combined, these three are the physical expression of obedience. They are the true outward, visible signs of an inward belief, the mercury in our spiritual thermometer.

If we truly are the Christian business that our letterhead, logos, and business cards suggest, it will be professed in our conduct. If not, all we did was say yes without ever showing up in the vineyard.

CHAPTER 10

GARDEN PRINCIPLE

Having arrived at the conclusion that God cares deeply about the businessperson but not the business itself, I faced an equally importunate question: Was my conclusion good news or bad news for our business? Should I be pleased that God does not care about business, or should it be cause for concern?

There are days when I would prefer Him not to meddle and other days when I want nothing more than to surround myself with supernatural intervention. Selfishly I desired both, but experience has taught me to lay aside my wants when pursuing truth. The two rarely coexist harmoniously. The other thing that experience has taught me is that truth can be found in some unlikely places. Who would have expected to find an enlightening business principle in the garden of Eden? That is where my investigation into this classic case of "good news, bad news" begins.

So much of what we do out of obedience is motivated by fear. It is true in every facet of life. Civil laws are obeyed because we fear the consequence of disobedience. Blue lights in my rearview mirror and the threat of a speeding ticket keep me right on the edge of what is legally allowed when I am driving my car. Fear of being grounded or losing cell phone privileges get our children home by curfew. Fear of termination gets our employees to work on time. Fear of audits and fines keep business owners within the confines of the tax code. In our society, fear of consequence is the greatest motivation for obedience. The same is largely true in religion as well, but not by God's design.

I have found that adherence due to fear of punishment is not limited to any particular religion, nor is it denominational within Christianity. As a young Catholic boy, fear of the confessional factored into every contemplated misdeed. As an adolescent looking for a spiritual connection and struggling with denominational issues, the fear of hell burdened my deliberations. As a Baptist adult, I take exception to some of the conventional fear-based methods used to prompt a relationship with Christ.

God's plan for obedience is not fear-based. It never has been, but it is easy to see how we have slipped into a fear-based mindset when you consider how often the word *fear* is used in Scripture. We need clarity because fear does have undeniable scriptural significance. Solomon wrote in the first chapter of Proverbs, "The fear of the Lord is the beginning of knowledge." In fact, the book of Proverbs attributes several desirable qualities to the fear of the Lord.

The fear of the Lord is the beginning of wisdom.
PROVERBS 9:10

The fear of the Lord prolongs life.
PROVERBS 10:27

In the fear of the Lord there is strong confidence,
And his children will have refuge.
The fear of the Lord is a fountain of life.
PROVERBS 14:26–27

The fear of the Lord leads to life.
PROVERBS 19:23

The book of Proverbs, all by itself, makes a strong argument for the many benefits of fearing the Lord. I would never challenge the belief that "fear of the Lord" cultivates significant spiritual qualities in our lives. The problem is that we tend to misunderstand—and then misplace—our fear. Living in the fear of the Lord and living fearfully are not the same. Those Scriptures from Proverbs are proof enough that the two fears are not synonymous. Living fearfully could not possibly bring about strong confidence. Living fearfully could not possibly be the fountain of life or the gateway to wisdom.

So, what kind of fear does bring strong confidence and life and wisdom? The only fear that can accomplish those things is the fear of the Lord. Living in the "fear of the Lord" means living in a manner that acknowledges the authority and power possessed by God. It is an awe that originates with an understanding of the great chasm that exists between His abilities and our own. It is a respect and a reverence that are the product of acknowledging God's unfathomable power, His knowledge, and His holiness. When we acknowledge and honor this great scale of difference between ourselves and God, we are compelled to act in obedience.

O Lord, You have searched me and known me.
You know when I sit down and when I rise up;
You understand my thought from afar.
You scrutinize my path and my lying down,
And are intimately acquainted with all my ways.
Even before there is a word on my tongue,

> *Behold, O Lord, You know it all.*
> *You have enclosed me behind and before,*
> *And laid Your hand upon me.*
> *Such knowledge is too wonderful for me;*
> *It is too high, I cannot attain to it.*
>
> **PSALM 139:1–6**

The psalmist David completely understood the vast difference between himself and the awesome God he served. He knew he could not attain the unfathomable level of his Creator. This knowledge brought life and wisdom and confidence. This understanding allowed David to clearly identify the true meaning of "the fear of the Lord."

> *I will give thanks to You, for I am fearfully*
> *and wonderfully made; Wonderful are Your*
> *works, And my soul knows it very well.*
>
> **PSALM 139:14**

We are not accustomed to seeing "fearfully" and "wonderfully" used together in this manner. Fear is supposed to be associated with awful or horrible. David was speaking of a different fear, a biblical fear, an awestruck respect and reverence. This component of our creation is unique to humans, a perspective that separates us from all other living things. All living things are wonderfully made by God, but we alone are both wonderfully and fearfully made. To understand this precept is to live in the "fear of the Lord" and is a critical element of our relationship with God. However, equally important is to understand that being fearfully made has no biblical connection to living fearfully.

God's plan for His relationship with us does not use fear as a fulcrum. His plan is love based, but like many other principles of God that organized religion assumed control over, this principle has been manipulated to better suit our own philosophy. We have constructed a fence built out of fear and declared it to be obedience. It is time to go back to the garden and refresh our perspective. From the very beginning, God's plan for obedience was clearly love based. That is what brings us to the garden of Eden in search of a significant business principle.

God spent five days creating the wonder, grandeur, enormity, and indescribable, indefinable intricacies of the universe. Creation is magnificent beyond words, beyond comprehension. It exceeds our ability to understand or explain. Every element of the universe, from the largest to the smallest, was wonderfully made, and Scripture says that it pleased God. It pleased God, but it did not yet fulfill Him. He desired something more.

> *Then God said, "Let Us make man in Our image, according to Our likeness."*
> **GENESIS 1:26**

God desired something that was both wonderfully and fearfully made. His creation of humans was singular in purpose. He desired fellowship, a communicable connection to all that had been created. God wanted to create something enough like Him that they could identify with who He is. The difference between humans and everything else He had created prior to man is summed up in "in Our image, according to Our likeness."

It has been debated for centuries as to what extent or depth we share the likeness of God, but I believe our free will forms the nucleus of the common image. When humanity's unique design is overlayed upon God's purpose for our creation, we get a clear picture of what He desires. It is unmistakable. Think about it for a moment: If all God desired was that we have a loving relationship with Him, that goal would have been easy to accomplish. By design, we could have been programmed for fellowship with God, hardwired not to deviate from that divine relationship. There would have been no joy, no delight for Him in that.

Instead, God created us in His likeness, giving us a free will. I truly believe that among the debated strands of similarity, our greatest likeness to God's image is our ability to choose to love Him. We fully satisfy God's ultimate desire each time we lovingly make that choice. Obedience motivated by love is the crown jewel of our free will. That is the only logical explanation for the forbidden tree.

> *Then the Lord God took the man and put him into the garden of Eden to cultivate it and keep it. The Lord God commanded the man, saying, "From any tree of the garden you may eat freely; but from the tree of the knowledge of good and evil you shall not eat, for in the day that you eat from it you shall surely die."*
>
> **GENESIS 2:15–17**

I can't help but wonder why that tree was even in the garden. If God's desire for man was fellowship, it makes no sense to place an object in the garden that could undermine that relationship. Remove the tree and you remove the possibility of broken fellowship. By intentionally placing the forbidden tree in the midst of the garden, God made it undeniably clear that free will and obedience are critical components of the fellowship He hopes to have with man. In fact, God takes it a step further. The tree that Adam and Eve were forbidden to eat from was intentionally very tempting.

> *The woman said to the serpent, "From the fruit of the trees in the garden we may eat; but from the fruit of the tree which is in the middle of the garden, God has said, 'You shall not eat from it or touch it, or you will die.'"*
> **GENESIS 3:2–3**

Look first at its location. The forbidden tree is not in some obscure, hard-to-reach corner of the garden. It is not hidden from view. God placed the tree in the middle of the garden. Again, I must ask why? When my children were younger, my wife and I would go to great lengths to place the things we did not want them to have out of sight or out of reach. It just makes sense. When our children grew older, we could prevent participation in undesirable internet activities by blocking access. As parents, we recognize those things that tempt our children into disobedience, and we do our best to remove them. God placed the tree in clear view. The forbidden tree was not only clearly seen and easily reached; it also bore desirable fruit.

> *When the woman saw that the tree was good for food, and that it was a delight to the eyes…*
> **GENESIS 3:6**

I am not at all well-traveled, but living near a large and diverse city, I have had the opportunity to visit some international grocery stores and markets. Food has always been a point of interest with me, so I am intrigued by the diets of the differing cultures. Walking the aisles, I have seen some curious sights. I am not a picky eater, willing to try most things, but I concede that there are foods in international markets that exceed my sense of culinary adventure. On multiple occasions I have come across items that I assume are considered edible, perhaps even delicacies, but I would never consider putting them in my mouth. It would be completely unnecessary to post a "Do Not Eat" sign above them. Conversely, there are other items that I have never tasted before that look delicious, and I immediately want to sample them. That is what happened in the garden. Eve's eyes got her taste buds to dancing. I've been there. The forbidden fruit was not just beautiful in appearance, and perhaps even fragrance, it was also good to eat. Why would God make it so appealing to both the eyes and the taste buds?

Before you answer, think about this: it does not stop there.

Eve also understood that the fruit had another desirable quality.

> *… and that the tree was desirable to make one wise.*
>
> **GENESIS 3:6**

Centrally located, easily reached, beautiful to look at, good to eat, desirable to make one wise, and yet, forbidden. Today, we would consider this to be entrapment. Why would God do that?

Our Creator does not want us to choose Him over the less desirable things life has to offer. For Adam and Eve not to eat of the forbidden fruit for any reason other than loving obedience would have brought no joy to God. If they did not eat from the tree because it was difficult to reach, or because the fruit was unappetizing, obedience would have little value.

The same is still true today. I call it the Garden Principle, and we seem to have lost sight of this truth. When I hear someone suggest that God took away all the things they held dear so they would be drawn close to Him, I want to cringe. How could it possibly be God's plan to take away money, recognition, health, security, relationships, or whatever else we might prefer above Him so He can, by default, steal the top ranking? Do we suppose that God is pleased when we choose Him only after all else is gone?

Absolutely not! He wants to be chosen over the best of creation. He wants our obedience to be the product of our desire to please the One we have chosen over every other thing creation has to offer. It was the driving force behind creating humanity "in Our image, according to Our likeness," the motive for the incredibly appealing design of the forbidden tree, and the crown jewel of our free will. It is the Garden Principle, and it has significant application to business.

Our human inclination is to obey out of our contemporary definition of fear. Even within the realm of religion, we have replaced fear of the Lord with fear of the consequence. It is only natural that we carry that same misdirected fear into our business or career. If we were to be completely honest, many of us attempt to operate our business or manage our career in a Christ-like manner for fear that if we don't, God may chastise us by hindering or perhaps even destroying our enterprise. We fret that He may use the failure of our business as a method of drawing us into obedience.

This notion is in direct conflict with what occurred in the garden. God has no more interest in destroying your business to win your obedience than He had in removing the forbidden tree. So, for everyone who is conducting business under the premise that God is watching with His hand on the plug, relax. If you find yourself operating on the fringe of biblical principles, stepping regularly over the boundary of obedience, and only stepping back out of fear of Holy retribution, I have what you will probably consider good news: God does not want to decrease your success in business to increase your desire to be obedient.

Now, here is the bad news: You are standing guard at the wrong gate. You are trying to protect something with no eternal value while leaving vulnerable the things that matter most. It is a testimony to our distorted perspective when we think that the thing of greatest value that God could take away from us is our business, while we willingly surrender our spiritual integrity and character. We end up living fearfully rather than living in the fear of the Lord. If your motive for Christian conduct in business is the fear of losing it, you have already lost something far greater. What you count as gain is loss. You are robbing yourself of strong confidence and the fountain of life.

There is a second form of misdirected fear. In motive, it is completely unlike the first. It is not intentional or self-serving. People who have this fear act in sincere obedience. They have no desire to bend obedience to suit business. This group understands the Garden Principle. They do not operate on the fringe of biblical principle. They are not looking back over their shoulder, hoping to step back in line just in time to avoid consequence. For them, spiritual integrity in business is the natural extension of their love relationship with the Lord. My wife is included in their number.

These are the people who are most likely to bristle at the theory that God does not care about business. It is much more difficult to defend my philosophy with this type of businessperson because, like my wife, their Christian character normally exceeds my own. I am not her equal with regard to loving obedience in the workplace, or any other place. The origin of her fear is based upon Scripture and is an extension of living in the fear of the Lord. The problem is that it extends too far.

Fear that is spiritually well intentioned ends up being misplaced. Fear of the Lord that should produce strong confidence can sadly result in living fearfully. How does this occur?

As contradictory as it may sound, there is a sincere humility associated with the strong confidence. There has to be. We are humbled when we submit to God's authority and acknowledge the enormous superiority of His power, wisdom, and holiness. This same humility caused David to declare that he could not attain to the height of God's knowledge. The confidence we possess does not rest in our own ability but in His. It is underwritten by the belief that God desires to empower us, to share His omnipotence with us.

> *Therefore humble yourselves under the mighty hand of God, that He may exalt you at the proper time.*
> **1 PETER 5:6**

> *I can do all things through Him who strengthens me.*
> **PHILIPPIANS 4:13**

It is biblical to walk in humility while drawing confidence in your ability, through Christ, to do all things. Unfortunately, even with a heart of sincere humility and a proper perspective of God's sovereign omnipotence, there is still room for misplaced fear. I believe this is the fear that forms the root of most people's objection to my business theory. For them, it is offensive for me to suggest that God does not care about business. My suggestion is perceived as haughty. To agree that God does not engage in the daily mechanics of business would be nothing less than arrogantly collaring God's glory. To suggest that a contract was not won or a sale not made by God's direct hand would selfishly rob God of His due. To not give credit to Him for a successful purchase or a creative process would be a vain elevation of self. Pride like that may elicit God's disappointment or, perhaps worse, His judgment. Would we willfully steal God's glory? This humility, though well-intentioned, can turn into misplaced fear.

What would lead us to believe that God's glory is attached to such fleeting and worldly activities? Again, it is a testimony to our wayward perspective. He may glory in the use of a balanced scale to make the sale, but the sale itself is not worthy. He may glory in the manner that the contract was written, but the contract itself is not worthy. The sale, the contract, the purchase, or any other number of transactions we may try to attach God's glory to are simply not worthy. We are underselling His glory. I do not wrest from God any measure of glory when I do not give Him credit for a worldly transaction. God's glory is reserved for much more glorious things.

The heavens declare the glory of God.
PSALM 19:1, NIV

*And suddenly there appeared with the angel a
multitude of the heavenly host praising God and saying,
"Glory to God in the highest,
And on earth peace among men with whom He is pleased."*
LUKE 2:13–14

*For God, who said, "Light shall shine out of darkness," is
the One who has shone in our hearts to give the Light of
the knowledge of the glory of God in the face of Christ.*
2 CORINTHIANS 4:6

The heavens, the gospel, the redemption of humanity, the face of Christ: those are the expressions of God's glory. How can my business deals be lumped in among them?

Do we increase God's glory by posting a quarterly profit?

If so, is His glory diminished if we lose money in business?

The daily mechanics of operating a business are neither instruments of nor expressions of God's glory. They fall woefully short of that magnificent honor. Business activities are the product of our intellectual design, our ambition, our free will, and we hope, our obedience. They are the result of being wonderfully and fearfully made. They are not the manifestation of God's glory.

The common rebuttal is that everything we do should be done to the glory of God, and its basis is found in 1 Corinthians.

> *Whether, then, you eat or drink or whatever*
> *you do, do all to the glory of God.*
> **1 CORINTHIANS 10:31**

The context of this verse makes that nature of it much more specific than the enormous generalization normally cast upon it. The passage deals largely with our attitude toward those who do not share all our spiritual behaviors. Look at how it begins:

> *All things are lawful, but not all things are*
> *profitable. All things are lawful, but not all things*
> *edify. Let no one seek his own good, but that of his*
> *neighbor. Eat anything that is sold in the meat market*
> *without asking questions for conscience' sake.*
> **1 CORINTHIANS 10:23–25**

The focus of this passage is to not offend others with the small nuances of our beliefs. God has a greater interest in the person than the incidental boundary of the dietary law. Let me give you an example.

Growing up as a Catholic, in a largely Catholic community, the school lunch menu always had a fish entrée on Fridays, designed to accommodate the Catholic tenet of not eating meat on Friday. In the seventh grade, my family relocated to Georgia. The school district was Protestant—overwhelmingly Southern Baptist—and fish was not the Friday entrée in the lunchroom. I could have refused to eat what was offered or I could have brought a peanut butter sandwich to school on Friday. My mother had the greater wisdom and instructed me to eat what was on the tray. She said, "God knows what is in the heart and will understand." If I had been spiritual enough to do it correctly, I would have eaten it to the glory of God as the book of Corinthians instructs, but in the seventh grade you lose sight of that. I ate it to the glory of pizza over fish!

Context of that very popular verse from Corinthians notwithstanding, I would never argue that all our words and actions—whether in church or in the office—should be done in such a manner, as if being done for God Himself. That is basic to what we believe as Christians, but being done to the glory of God is not the same as glorifying God. The things we do that have no eternal value are done to our own glory. That sounds bad, but it's really not. Don't beat yourself up.

It is not inherently evil that many of our actions and achievements contribute to our own glory. In most cases, we don't give ourselves the glory but others place it on us. We walk in a physical world, and the world applies that glory based upon its own value system. It is not a spiritual indictment upon you or me if the world glorifies us for the things we have been able to accomplish. We just need to be vigilant not to slip into that same mindset. We also need to remain mindful of the great chasm, the great scale of difference between God's glory and our own. Consider the enormous wealth and respect that Solomon obtained in his lifetime when you read the words of Jesus.

> *"Consider the lilies, how they grow: they neither toil nor spin; but I tell you, not even Solomon in all his glory clothed himself like one of these."*
> **LUKE 12:27**

Jesus was not being critical of Solomon's glory. By granting wisdom, God had made it possible for Solomon to amass such wealth. Jesus was simply trying to illustrate the enormous difference between the things that glorify man and those that glorify God. Our physical possessions and mortal achievements, regardless of how numerous, cannot even compare to a field of lilies.

I can't help but chuckle at my own foolishness over the number of times I have driven home from work thinking that I had elevated God's glory with an outstanding business achievement while I zoomed past highway medians full of wildflowers. Yet the flowers, which went largely unnoticed by me, glorified God way beyond anything I could accomplish in business. I am a silly man.

The fact that God is not concerned with business is neither good news nor bad news. It should not excite us or disappoint us. However, we should respond by analyzing our business model, evaluating our attitude, considering our approach, redirecting our focus, and perhaps setting fresh goals.

Why?

Because even though it is not found in an accounting ledger, a spreadsheet, or a marketing plan, your business still has a divine purpose. You have a kingdom responsibility.

CHAPTER 11

WHAT THEN?

The root misconception of most people who dismiss my perspective of biblical business is that they think I believe business falls outside the boundaries of God's will. That is absolutely not the case. I know now beyond any shadow of doubt that what I am doing professionally is exactly what God would have me to do with my life. Chances are that you feel the same way. Your business may fall smack-dab in the center of God's divine will for your life. Your chosen career, your livelihood may be the exact path that God desires for you.

What, then?

How can I believe that God does not care about business when that very business may place me in the center of His will? It is a logical question, but the answer is quite simple. We tend to place our focus upon the task rather than the purpose. We consider the business task to be the significant component while God has set his sight upon what He hopes to achieve for His kingdom's sake. There can be a huge difference between the two.

Moses was in God's will when he was in Pharaoh's court, but Pharaoh's court was not what God had an interest in. The same is true of

Moses's time as a shepherd in the wilderness. He was in God's will, but increasing the flock was not the intent. God did not place Moses in that position to create the largest, highest quality, most efficiently run flock in the region. Moses could have set his focus upon the task and never approached the burning bush to discover his purpose.

There is an interesting side note and real concern in this whole task-versus-purpose discussion. You will recall from the third and fourth chapter of Exodus, Moses tried very hard to talk his way out of God's purpose. It makes me wonder how many times I have had a God encounter, but unlike Moses, I refused the purpose and continued to focus on the business task. Somebody needs to tend the sheep, right? It sounds like something I would say.

Joseph had a similar situation in the court of an earlier Pharaoh. His was no small role. Joseph was literally given charge over all of Egypt.

> *Then Pharaoh said to His servants, "Can we find a man like this, in whom is a divine spirit?" So Pharaoh said to Joseph, "Since God has informed you of all this, there is no one so discerning and wise as you are. You shall be over my house, and according to your command all my people shall do homage; only in the throne I will be greater than you." Pharaoh said to Joseph, "See, I have set you over all the land of Egypt."*
> **GENESIS 41:38–41**

Three points cannot be argued. First, Joseph was in God's will. Even Pharaoh recognized how God's hand was upon Joseph. Second, Joseph's task was to rule over all of Egypt. Third, ruling over Egypt was not God's purpose for placing Joseph in a position to find favor with

Pharaoh. The task, the business to be done, the day-to-day mechanics of ruling over Egypt was not God's motive or His concern. He left that part to Joseph.

Was Peter in God's will as a fisherman? Do you think it was for the purpose of creating a commercial fishing empire? It seems unlikely since Jesus called him out of that business on what was probably the most lucrative day of his fishing career. Peter's boating knowledge and fishing skills are a common thread woven throughout the Gospels. Peter's time as a fisherman was preparation, and it was a platform for the gospel. The fishing was secondary.

Our livelihood may place us within God's will for our life, but the task itself is not why we are there. I know God's kingdom is not made better by the manufacture of steel products, but the manufacture of steel products is where I have been placed. So there is where I will use the God-given attributes of my intellectual, creative, design, and free will to make a living, but it is also the platform from which I am expected to influence God's kingdom. My kingdom influence will not be measured by *Forbes*, nor will yours.

I truly believe that in my lifetime nobody has grasped that principle better than Truett Cathy. As I stated earlier, Chick-fil-A's slogan is, "We didn't invent the chicken, just the chicken sandwich." However, inventing the chicken sandwich was not God's concern. No matter how delicious, God is not glorified by a boneless, perfectly fried, all-meat chicken breast on a delightfully soft bun, garnished with a slice of pickle. He is not even glorified by the fact that the Cathy family still defies business logic and chooses to close their restaurants on Sunday, a decision that over time will cost in the billions of dollars. What does glorify God in the example of Truett Cathy?

It all boils down to this: A man, wonderfully and fearfully made, willfully chose to be obedient even when tempted by the best this world has to offer. It was a choice both he and his son Dan made. It is a choice Dan's son Andrew continues to make. God's pleasure is with Cathy men, not the *Closed* sign. His delight is the obedience of the one created in His image. His delight is in the one who recognizes Him as Lord.

You may argue that the Sunday closure is a testimony. I see that point, but the local Department of Motor Vehicles is closed on Sunday too. Try to get a building permit on Sunday or mail a letter with the United States Postal Service. They are all closed on Sunday, but it gives no witness. It gives no testimony to God. I think it is unlikely that people drive past the *Closed* sign at Chick-fil-A on Sunday and are compelled to attend church as a result. They don't pull into the parking lot and give praise to God for the chicken sandwich they could not buy. In truth, the people it has the most profound impact upon are those like me, who already claim to have a spiritual relationship with God. Ironically enough, we are the very ones who drive past Mr. Cathy's restaurant on our way to eat at some other establishment that is open on Sunday. We applaud his commitment and call it a testimony, but we don't feel spiritually compelled to participate in it.

I have never met Truett Cathy and would not presume to completely understand his motive, but based upon what I have read, I believe his decision to close on Sunday was nothing greater than, and nothing less than, a personal conviction to be obedient. If something larger than that comes of it, it falls into the category of feeding the five thousand. God uses obedience to do a greater work.

As much as it pains my mortal, usually hungry flesh to say it, there will be no Chick-fil-A store in heaven. It is an earthly treasure. When I arrive at my eternal home, I will not get to enjoy the most delicious chicken sandwich ever invented, but I do hope to meet the man who invented it. I would love to sit and listen to God and Truett Cathy talk, just to see if the topic of business ever comes up. My guess is no.

What, then? What will they talk about? What is the connection between Mr. Cathy's business and God's will? It is the same as the connection between Joseph's, Moses's, Solomon's, and Peter's business and God's will. It is an opportunity to be obedient while functioning within our intellectual design and free will. It is the opportunity to extend our obedient influence to all those who look to us for leadership or depend upon us for their livelihood. It is the opportunity for us to function fairly and honestly as a sincere expression of living confidently in the fear of the Lord. It is the ideal platform to fulfill the two greatest commands.

> *And one of them, a lawyer, asked Him a question, testing Him, "Teacher, which is the great commandment in the Law?" And He said to him, "'You shall love the Lord your God with all your heart, and with all your soul, and with all your mind.' This is the great and foremost commandment. The second is like it, 'You shall love your neighbor as yourself.' On these two commandments depend the whole Law and the Prophets."*
> **MATTHEW 22:35–40**

What, then?

If we fail in the greatest, we have little hope for the second. If we fail in the second, we have not satisfied the greatest. More than anything else, it comes down to people. God cares about people. That is what He sees. People are the connection between God's will and our business.

> *"Nearly every moment of every day we have the opportunity to give something to someone else—our time, our love, our resources. I have always found more joy in giving when I did not expect anything in return."*
>
> **S. TRUETT CATHY**[4]

If I ever do get the chance to listen in, I'll bet this is what Mr. Cathy and God will be talking about.

---

[4]. Bryan Cronan, "How Chick-fil-A's S. Truett Cathy Pioneered the Charitable Business," The Christian Science Monitor, September 8, 2014, https://www.csmonitor.com/Business/2014/0908/How-Chick-Fil-A-s-S.-Truett-Cathy-pioneered-the-charitable-business.

CHAPTER 12

AMALIA

Quirky is a word that self-conscious people use to describe their own strange habits or ideas. I confess to having some quirky ideas when it comes to machinery. Mechanical things interest me—all of them. They have for my entire life. Mechanical things and machinery comprise my core competency at work. They are intertwined into most of my tinkering hobbies and form the root of my love for automobile racing.

Most people believe high-speed wrecks are the big draw in NASCAR, and that may be the case for many, but my fascination is a combustion engine that can turn 9,000 RPMs for five hundred miles. I am amazed how a half pound of air pressure in a single tire can dramatically improve, or destroy, a car's handling. Minutely small increments of measure in size, weight, or temperature can create enormous swings in performance. It is entertaining and interesting at the same time. I am that guy who takes things apart just to see how they work. (Sometimes I am even able to put them back together.)

I love machinery, but that in itself is not unusual. The thing that makes my interest a bit quirky is that I fantasize that machines have mechanical souls. Nothing spiritual, of course. I am not that strange. I am talking about "soul" as in an individual identity, a unique mechanical personality. Just like people — no two are exactly the same. They may share similar components and have the same model number, but each has its own serial number, and each has unique idiosyncrasies. The mechanical soul makes it possible for me to develop a connection to an otherwise inanimate object.

I name all the major machines in my life and grow attached to them much the same way that you would a pet. It is especially true of my vehicles. Over the last thirty-five years, I have driven just four vehicles. All were trucks. The first, named "Slick"; the second, "Angus Bull"; then "Buster"; and now "Bernard." Combined, I accumulated nearly a million miles on them. I suspect that Bernard and I will be together for at least ten years. Strange? No, just quirky.

At work I am surrounded by machinery. In our manufacturing facility we have many pieces of equipment. I depend more on some than on others. A handful of them are absolutely critical in our day-to-day operations. One such piece of equipment is an 1,100-ton hydraulic press. It is a massive, complex, and at times cantankerous machine, and we depend upon it heavily. On one particular occasion, it quit running and the maintenance team was having a difficult time discerning and resolving the issue. We had been out of operation for three days, and the lost production time was threatening our customer's assembly plant. We had been reaching out and consulting with outside repair specialists to try and correct the issue, but each attempt failed to correct the problem. Late on a Friday evening after yet another failed attempt, I went out to the press to get an update from an associate whom I will call Raul, the press operator. He had been very involved in the troubleshooting process, and I could see it had taken its toll upon him. His countenance was sullen.

"Any luck, Raul?" I asked, knowing full well the answer.

"No," Raul said. "It still does not work. I don't know."

Raul is of Hispanic descent. He speaks functional English with a heavy accent. What his speech lacks technically is more than made up for with emotion. I clearly understood his last comment to be one of despair.

"Have you ever named this machine?" I asked, pointing at the disabled press.

Raul looked at me with an expression best described as disbelief, veiled by an attempt not to be disrespectful to me. What struck me most was the spark of curiosity in his eyes.

"Raul," I said, "machines have mechanical souls."

The veil of respect washed off, and I was speaking into the face of sheer disbelief.

"If you want this machine to respond, you need to develop a more personal connection with it."

Raul was not sure whether I was serious or just playing with him. I have a reputation for such—blame it on quirky.

"Raul, get your cell phone out."

Now he knew I was serious. I had just instructed him to do something that would have otherwise gotten him fired. Cell phone use on the manufacturing floor is one of my pet peeves. It is as unsafe as it is unproductive.

"This press was built in Sweden, and something about it makes me believe it is female," I said. "I want you to go online and search for Swedish girl names."

Raul hesitated, but I coaxed him, and together we perused a listing of popular girl names in Sweden. After a few minutes, he and I settled upon "Amalia." According to the information we read, it means "industrious." The name was perfect, and I went through a proper introduction.

"Raul, you can't just come in here every day and demand things of Amalia with the expectation that she requires nothing in return," I said. "Show your appreciation, communicate, encourage, and develop a relationship with her. She is industrious. She wants to work. She just needs to know that her contribution is recognized and appreciated. Give her efforts some meaning besides your own gain."

He peered at me again to make certain I was not trying to make him look foolish.

"Go ahead, Raul. Tell her."

Hesitantly, Raul expressed his appreciation to Amalia for her past service, and he politely requested her further cooperation. He spoke as if to a person.

"Very good, Raul. That is a great start. Now, how about you turn Amalia off for the night and let her think about what was said? Tomorrow we will come back ready to work through this together."

As I drove home that evening, I was dumbfounded by my own stupidity.

"How could I have been so blind?"

I had just encouraged Raul... no, I had more than encouraged. I had ushered Raul into a relationship with a piece of machinery that was deeper and more personal than the relationship I had with him. The principle I taught Raul, the same principle I applied to all the major mechanical devices in my life, I had failed to apply to people. Raul had been with us for nearly two years, and I knew very little about him other than the things he did at work, the things he did to afford the company gain.

Did he have a girlfriend?
Was it possible that he was married?
Had a child?

What were his hobbies, his goals, his career aspirations?
Where was he originally from?
Was his family still there?

I did not even know Raul's last name. I was ashamed. Each day when I came to work, I either directly or indirectly placed demands upon Raul with very little connection to him personally. I expected something more than the minimum effort from him and offered nothing in return except his wage. Any manager or owner could do that much. I had been denying him the things that I asked him to give to Amalia: encouragement, appreciation, and recognition. More questions popped into my head.

What did Raul think of me?
Did he perceive me as someone uninterested in anything other than generating revenue?
Did Raul believe I had no interest in his life away from the workplace?
Did he think I could only appreciate his existence if he was constantly efficient at his job?

He only knew me as the guy who wanted answers.

"When are you going to be finished?"

"How many parts did you make?"

"What are you going to make next?"

"How long will that take?"

I was the guy who ranted about cell phones and preached constantly about productivity and parts per hour. I did not want him to view me as that guy. As I continued to think about it, I sank deeper. It was not just Raul. There were at least a dozen more people on the manufacturing floor just like him, people whose names showed up each morning on the daily production reports, and I knew them only by how many parts they could produce in a shift.

How could I have missed the mark so badly? I could not wait to get back to work the next morning to correct my error. Raul and I had our first real, nonbusiness-related chat. I think it surprised him more than when I told him that machines had souls. When he and I were through, I had similar conversations with several other members of the production team. I made connections.

If we desire to do God's will in business, people are where we must start.

> *"The second is like it, 'You shall love your neighbor as yourself.' On these two commandments depend the whole Law and the Prophets."*
>
> **MATTHEW 22:39–40**

God may leave the operation of business in our hands, but He delights when business is done within the framework of obedience to the two greatest commandments. People should be the priority in any business or career that claims an association with God. Every other act of obedience springs forth from the way we treat other people. If we seek God's favor, if we desire to reflect Him in our business efforts, then people are where we must place our focus. That is why I said that the way the contract is written is what He cares about. The balance on the scale is much more important to God then the size of the transaction. What are our policies and our attitudes toward associates and employees? Equally important, what are our policies toward our competitors?

> *Do not rejoice when your enemy falls,*
> *And do not let your heart be glad when he stumbles;*
> *Or the Lord will see it and be displeased.*
>
> **PROVERBS 24:17–18**

> *But love your enemies, and do good, and lend,*
> *expecting nothing in return; and your reward will*
> *be great, and you will be sons of the Most High; for*
> *He Himself is kind to ungrateful and evil men.*

LUKE 6:35

I am not just supposed to have a concern for those within our company. I am also to have a concern, a love, for our competitors. I am instructed to do "good" to them. This seems contrary to profitable business practices. It is inconsistent with the traditional business model. It is not the method by which business empires have been built in the past. The accepted norm is to develop a strategy to crush your competition. If it can't be done fairly, then find some other means. Loving your competitor is not part of the contemporary equation for succeeding in the business world, unless you choose to operate in the fear of the Lord. While the business world is adding up the things that moths eat and rust destroys, God continues to focus on people. For us, focusing upon people should not be a business decision. It should be a personal decision to live in obedience.

When I got to the point of being able to recognize the importance of people over profit, my mindset became, "Lord, provide me enough revenue that I can do some good." It was a case of simple economics. If God would assist me in my effort to create greater profit in business, I would have the resources to make an impact upon people, similar to those that businessmen like Truett Cathy have made.

Again, I erred in my reckoning. We deceive ourselves believing that we must have billion-dollar companies to fulfill the intent of the greatest commandments. The truth is that Mr. Cathy already had the "love your neighbor as yourself" heart when he opened his first small restaurant just south of Atlanta. You don't need a billion-dollar company to affect lives. You just need to be obedient.

> *When He went ashore, He saw a large crowd, and felt compassion for them and healed their sick. When it was evening, the disciples came to Him and said, "This place is desolate and the hour is already late; so send the crowds away, that they may go into the villages and buy food for themselves." But Jesus said to them, "They do not need to go away; you give them something to eat!" They said to Him, "We have here only five loaves and two fish." And He said, "Bring them here to Me." Ordering the people to sit down on the grass, He took the five loaves and the two fish, and looking up toward heaven, He blessed the food, and breaking the loaves He gave them to the disciples, and the disciples gave them to the crowds, and they all ate and were satisfied. They picked up what was left over of the broken pieces, twelve full baskets. There were about five thousand men who ate, besides women and children.*
>
> **MATTHEW 14:14–21**

The spiritual moral to this story is that God does not need nearly as much as what we calculate to be necessary to accomplish His goals. Jesus did not require the disciples to come up with the food needed to feed five thousand men. He did not even show them that He had enough to feed everyone before instructing them to start handing it out. Regardless of whether you have thousands of employees or just one, you have what is necessary to be an instrument of the Lord. If you love your neighbor as yourself, you have the opportunity to make an impact. God did not need Mr. Cathy to show up with 1,500 restaurants. That single little "Dwarf House" south of Atlanta and a heart for people was enough.

The principle of God multiplying resources to do His work is one of the arguments that people use to substantiate the claim that God does care about business. The belief is that He brings about increase to further His Kingdom. It is a belief that is true on the back end but errs on the front.

While it is true that God multiplies the resources we offer to further His Kingdom, He simply does not concern Himself with bringing about the increase. God leaves that task to us. It is my job; it is your job. It is the task of anyone who owns and manages a business.

Chick-fil-A grew to its present size because the Cathy family works hard, makes good business decisions, sells a quality product, and offers superior customer service. If they fail to do those things, their business will also fail. God is not growing their business, nor will he grow my business or yours. That is not God's task. It is our own. We must do that ourselves. If it is done in His will, if it is built upon biblical principles and operated in the fear of the Lord, then He will multiply what it generates and use it for His kingdom's sake. I am certain there are still those who will disagree with me on this point. I accept that. However, a world filled with millions of starving people compels me to maintain my belief.

In Matthew's account of the feeding of the five thousand, Scripture states that Jesus saw the multitude and was filled with compassion. He instructed His disciples not to send them away but to feed them. Those people had only been with Him one day without food. Most had probably missed no more than a meal. Hungry, sure; starving, not really. Jesus felt compassion and wanted the people fed anyway. He used His miraculous omnipotent power to turn five loaves and two fish into enough food to satisfy the appetite of the thousands who were there. When they finished eating, there were twelve baskets of leftovers.

I believe Jesus is as compassionate today as He was then. I must believe the Lord's heart breaks that people all over the world go to sleep at night with hunger gnawing at their stomachs. If you believe the biblical account in Matthew, then you must also believe that God, who feels compassion for humankind, has the authority and miraculous power to speak enough food into existence to feed the hungry.

So why are people starving?

Who does He expect to feed them?

The answer of course is us. You and I, humanity—it is our task to feed the hungry. Just as Jesus told His disciples.

> *But Jesus said to them, "They do not need to go away; you give them something to eat!"*
> **MATTHEW 14:16**

God's desire is that we feel compassion and feed the hungry.

What does this have to do with whether or not God cares about business?

We have no problem agreeing that God stands back and entrusts us with such a significant and life-threatening issue as feeding the hungry, yet we bristle at the idea that He would leave the production of widgets or the sale of sandwiches to our own devices. Do you see the folly in that?

Allow me to substitute my own petition in place of the disciples'.

> *"Lord, there is so much that I could accomplish, so many good deeds that could be done, if only I had the revenue. Grow my*

business and increase my sales; help me become more profitable. Use this business to impact other people's lives."

"You can take care of growing that business yourself. What do you have that I can use right now?"

"Not much, Lord. Just a handful of employees and a small building."

"That's good enough; now impact a life."

Do something good for someone else. It doesn't have to be monetary. Encourage, compliment, express gratitude, or lend a hand. These acts of kindness and appreciation are things that everybody is capable of, and they don't require a budget. Your actions will define you in the workplace. Find ways, even small ways, of letting them know that you appreciate what they have contributed. The wage is compensation for our associates' labor, but I am fully aware they can make a wage at other places. I want to express my gratitude that they chose to labor with us. Small acts can make a big difference. By our nature, we all want to feel appreciated. This desire extends beyond fair wage. I like to believe that my contribution to the success of our company has value beyond the monetary compensation. You are probably no different, and neither are those who work with us.

As a businessperson, opportunities come up continuously throughout the day. They are the loaves and fishes that we can use to make a difference. If we do not consciously make an effort to seize these opportunities, they will slip away.

One of my favorite passages parallels the Truett Cathy quote. I believe it to be applicable in every area of our lives, but I particularly like its application to business.

> *Do not withhold good from those to whom it is due,*
> *When it is in your power to do it.*
>
> **PROVERBS 3:27**

Your position in the business world often makes it well within your power to do good for someone else. We pass up opportunity after opportunity believing we do not have enough resources to make a difference, we are not big enough, or we don't have enough influence. We put it off for a later time. As a result, we miss out on all the things that we could do, planning the things that we would do. You do not need to think globally or even regionally. Start on the other side of your office door. Set your focus on the people around you, your employees, your associates, suppliers, customers, and, yes, even your competitors. In those relationships and those interactions you will discover and fulfill God's will for your business week. That is the area of business He has an interest in. It is one of the very few things that you can do in the workplace that qualifies as a Kingdom treasure.

There are two interesting side notes:

1. Amalia cooperated the next morning for Raul. She was back up and producing parts by noon on Saturday. I know that this was largely a coincidence, but it was a perfectly timed one. I am not viewed as quite so "quirky" anymore.

2. I learned that Raul is not married, but he does have a girlfriend. He is originally from Mexico. Raul is the youngest of six children and all his family still resides in Mexico City. He is very happy to be living in this country, but at times he misses his family. The English was not perfect, but the

emotion was clear. I thanked him for working with us. I count Raul as a friend.

CHAPTER 13

DRINKING THE RAIN

So much of my life is spent at work, both physically and mentally. It would trouble me to see my life presented in a pie chart. If you are operating or managing a business, my guess is that you are the same way. Another guess is that as a Christian you have wondered if you are doing what you should with your time. We are given just one short trip across this planet, one shot at life, one chance to get it right in the sight of God and in the presence of those we love. I came to the point of needing to know the spiritual relevance of my labor.

I was certain from years of study that God expected His followers to not only be workers, but exemplary workers. I got that. I think most of us do, but there had to be more. If I really was doing what God would have me to do, some greater gain, some larger purpose had to be part of satisfying that requirement. The portion of my life that business occupied was too large to be ignored from a spiritual perspective. I needed answers.

That is what started me on this journey. I wanted to understand how God felt about the thing that was consuming so much of my time and energy. I wanted to know that in the sight of God, my short trip across the planet was not being squandered. I was hoping to get confirmation that God had an active, vested interest in the success of what I was doing with the majority of my waking hours. What I was looking for is not exactly what I found.

To restate my conclusion, God does not care about business. This assertion I know troubles some of those who hear it. When I started out on this quest, that conclusion would have troubled me. However, my investigation has led me to another unexpected conclusion. I am okay with the idea that God does not care about business. In fact, as I said earlier, I am blessed by it.

How can I be blessed by the fact that God does not care about that which occupies most of my waking hours? It makes perfect sense when you realize where God's care is actually being applied. Two illustrations separated by forty-five years will help me explain.

I am not familiar with today's method of elementary school grading, but way back in my elementary school days, report cards were twofold. One half of the report consisted of subject letter grades—A through F. On the other half were your conduct grades. I have three older sisters, all of them much more intelligent than me, and they set a precedent of outstanding report cards. When I entered elementary school, my parents' expectation was that I would do the same. Though not able to achieve my sisters' standards, I did manage to put together some pretty good report cards. I remember bringing home a report that just missed perfection, one B and all the rest As. It was certain to please Mom and Dad—or so I thought. But Dad's expression as he read the report made it clear that something did not sit well with him.

"What is this 'N'?"

On the conduct side of the report card was a long list of evaluations related to classroom behavior. Typically, they were not egregious or harmful actions. Most were subjective at best.

Pays attention in class.

Follows instructions.

Shows respect to classmates.

Does not talk out of turn.

Good manners.

Courteous.

The conduct report was also assigned letter grades, but it was not the normal A through F. Conduct was graded with its own set of letters.

S: Satisfactory

N: Needs improvement

U: Unsatisfactory

Evidently, somewhere among the long laundry list of S behavior, my dad spotted an N. In my mind, the N was insignificant, not worthy of mention. I could not even recollect which of the dozens of silly evaluations my teacher felt was lacking. It was a bit confusing really. I would have thought that getting a B rather than an A was a much bigger problem. That was not the case, but I fought back.

"Dad, Ns are not bad. Us are bad. I did not get any Us."

"Wrong, son," my dad said. "Ns are bad. N means your conduct needs to improve. 'Needs to improve' means that it is currently not as good as it should be. N is unacceptable."

I knew better than to argue out loud, but in my head I was screaming, "Are you kidding me? I almost made straight As and you are going to bust my chops over a stupid N for some goofy little thing the teacher thinks I need to improve?"

I do not recall my dad's exact words, but I have not forgotten the gist of his message. Grades may rank me, but my conduct defines me. Conduct was the window into my heart, my integrity, my honor, and equally importantly, my heritage. He made a point of the fact that my public behavior reflected upon our entire family and, more specifically, him and my mother. Like it or not, I represented something larger than myself. Opinions would be formed and conclusions drawn about my dad based upon my conduct. What I felt was secondary to scholastic performance was primary in the sight of my father. He valued integrity over intelligence. Dad was certain that I possessed enough knowledge for the grades to work themselves out if I made my conduct a priority.

Fast-forward forty-five years. I was in my father-in-law's office. John is a godly man, and I respect his spiritual perspectives even though I know they differ from mine regarding business. During this particular meeting, we were discussing two of my projects that were in distress. One was experiencing mechanical issues, while the other had dragged on past its scheduled delivery date. Both were weighing heavily upon my mind. As I was leaving, I told him that it would be a good day if we could complete the development on the tardy job and solve the mechanical issues on the other.

"Well then," John said, "that is exactly what I will pray for, even though I know you disagree."

I tend to second-guess my opinions when they contradict those of people whom I respect. Smiling almost apologetically, I thanked him for the prayers and went about the business of trying to accomplish my two objectives. As I labored that day, I wondered if a prayer for me to finish was indeed one that God felt compelled to oblige. By the end of the day, it seemed apparent that the answer to that question was no. After ten hours of persistent effort, neither project proved successful. Neither showed much more promise than they had the day before.

What happened? I know that John had done exactly what he said he would do: he prayed for the success of those two projects. Scripture makes it clear that God hears our faithful prayers.

> *But know that the Lord has set apart the godly man for Himself; The Lord hears when I call to Him.*
>
> **PSALM 4:3**

God heard John's prayer, so I considered the possible explanations. Perhaps it simply was not God's will for me to succeed that day. If that is the case, what purpose do our prayers serve? If God is going to carry out His predetermined will regardless of our supplication, what is the sense in praying for anything other than God's will be done—even that prayer seems unnecessary if God is going to do His will anyway? As much as I appreciated the prayers of a godly man, they would seem to be ineffective if they fall outside of God's will.

Maybe the problem was a lack of faith on my part. Maybe John's prayer was on point, and God denied the request because I was hesitant to believe that He was concerned about a couple of troubled machines. The problem with that explanation is that I do not question God's omnipotent power and His ability to do whatever He chooses. At any point in time during that day, I am convinced He could have dropped the stars out of the heavens if He so desired. I believe He holds my next breath and that the sun cannot rise without

His permission. I do not question the unmatched, mind-boggling power and authority of God. There are certainly people with faith greater than my own, but I do not see my lack of faith as the deterrent.

The explanation that I kept coming back to was that God had no concern for those two specific projects. They each fell into the category of those things that are left to my control. Their failure was my doing. Had they worked, their success would also have been my doing. The more relevant prayer is not that I succeed in the task, but that I succeed in the handling of the task. There is a considerable difference in the two, and I set myself on an errant course that morning in John's office. I had stated that it would be a "good day" if my two troubled projects achieved success. By the end of the day, neither had. Did that therefore mean that it was not a good day? Are my days supposed to be defined by my work achievements? Is that my measuring stick?

Is it God's measuring stick? I had set my focus upon the things that rank me rather than those that define me. What are the criteria for a "good day" at work?

In my Father's eyes, a good day at work is not dependent upon my business achievements. A good day is a day of obedience, a day of conduct that is consistent with the relationship I profess to have with Him. He is pleased when I do well with the things that define my character rather than those that rank me professionally.

That means that I can have a good day in His sight even if I fail in my business objectives. That realization is thrilling to me. I am blessed by it. Every day at work can be a good day. Machines may break down, projects may lose money, delivery dates may be missed, bids rejected, and the people around me may have a constant string of unexpected requests, but I still have the opportunity to have a good day. We could experience enormous growth and become a

Fortune 500 company, or we could be auctioned on the courthouse steps—either one would be fine with God. All He is concerned with is how we conducted ourselves on the way there. It is liberating to begin each business day with that mindset.

I have been equipped by God with the tools necessary to provide for myself and my family. I have been given life and health. I have the ability to acquire knowledge. I am able to reason and gain understanding. I have access to wisdom. Each day I carry all these tools with me to work determined to prove myself an exemplary laborer. My business success or failure each day, my ranking among others will be dependent upon those tools, but it can be a fickle and fleeting roller coaster ride of emotional highs and lows.

I also go to work each day determined to act with integrity and character to be a reflection of my spiritual Father. That is what will define my character in business. It is not a scale established by humans. It is God's business scale, and it is neither fickle nor fleeting, paying out guaranteed dividends. It is where God places His concern. It is His measuring stick for a "good day," and He delights in it.

Understanding and applying this principle will change your goals in business. It will change the way you look at your workweek, and it has the potential to define your trip across this planet. There are times when I fail, days when I fall short or lose sight, but I no longer leave for work in the morning fixed upon making money or growing the business. I go to work to drink the rain.

> *For ground that drinks the rain which often falls on it*
> *and brings forth vegetation useful to those for whose*
> *sake it is also tilled, receives a blessing from God;*
>
> **HEBREWS 6:7**

In this verse I have discovered my purpose in work. I have uncovered the eternal significance of my mortal labor and finally grasped what I believe to be God's perspective upon the large portion of my life that is given to business. I am now confident that I know how He grades my performance, and I understand the measuring stick for good days and bad. The undeniable, inescapable, and glorious truth is that my labor has spiritual purpose and therefore it has meaning far beyond the manufacture of sheet metal parts. It is intended that your business, your career, likewise have spiritual purpose.

In this Scripture from Hebrews, I want you to think of business as "the ground." It is the equivalent of a farmer's land. The farmer plows the ground, and you ply your trade, whatever it may be. Your business or career is the ground from which you draw your harvest. Just like the hardworking farmer, we are exhorted in Scripture to be laborers—diligent, exemplary, and working as if to the Lord.

Therefore, the word *tilled* is important to the meaning and application of this biblical precept and should not be overlooked in this verse. Tilling the ground is an act of labor. Prior to modern farming and the use of tractors, tilling was a physical, strenuous act. When this verse is viewed from a business perspective, it seems evident that we are to have our hand upon the plow. Labor is expected of us, but tilling involves more than just brute force. Those who have worked the land understand the importance of knowledge. There is a proper time, a wrong way and right way to apply the plow. A successful crop requires both the farmer's labor and his expertise. Not all fields yield the same harvest, even those that are side by side. The plants must be tended, and the farmer's knowledge and willingness to work have a great impact upon the success or failure of his crop. As an adolescent, I spent my summers working on a farm in southeastern Wisconsin. I have seen firsthand the value of well-tended fields. I understand the importance of good decision-making and hard work.

Equally important is self-discipline. Tilling is not like harvesting. It produces no immediate yield. It is a preparation. Tilling does not put vegetables in the bushel basket. You cannot sell tilling at the market. Farmers must have the discipline to do the difficult groundwork in anticipation of the future harvest.

> *Go to the ant, O sluggard,*
> *Observe her ways and be wise,*
> *Which, having no chief,*
> *Officer or ruler,*
> *Prepares her food in the summer*
> *And gathers her provision in the harvest.*
>
> **PROVERBS 6:6–8**

> *He who tills his land will have plenty of food,*
> *But he who follows empty pursuits*
> *will have poverty in plenty.*
>
> **PROVERBS 28:19**

Tilling defines our contribution to the vegetation that is brought forth. It is a critical component of this biblical business equation, but even when we are obedient in the biblical instruction to till, something more is required. The farmer must have rain. His crops need it, and his livelihood depends upon it. The rain is out of the farmer's control. Watering the crops is a God thing, arriving on God's timing and falling where He desires. Without the God-given rain, the farmer toils in vain.

I am not in the farming business, so my success does not literally depend upon the rain. It does, however, depend upon some metaphorical rain, those things that occur out of my control, those things that are not by my hand—God things. The encouragement we get from Hebrews 6:7 is that the rain "often falls on" the ground. God continually pours out upon us those things that allow us not to toil in vain. Like the rain, they are things that I cannot manufacture or negotiate. They are not contracts, profits, sales, promotions, business models, or anything of the sort. The rain that God sends to us in business is wisdom and discernment. These are qualities that are God-given.

> *But if any of you lacks wisdom, let him ask of God, who gives to all generously and without reproach, and it will be given to him.*
> **JAMES 1:5**

> *For the Lord gives wisdom;*
> **PROVERBS 2:6**

> *Behold, You desire truth in the innermost being, And in the hidden part You will make me know wisdom.*
> **PSALM 51:6**

> *You have dealt well with Your servant, O Lord, according to Your word. Teach me good discernment and knowledge, For I believe in Your commandments.*
> **PSALM 119:65–66**

Hebrews 6:7 makes it clear that God causes these things that we cannot manufacture to fall upon us often. The instruction is to drink them in, absorb them. It is not automatic. Not all ground drinks the rain, and it certainly does not do it equally in all places. The ground that most readily drinks the rain is ground that has been prepared, tilled, and cultivated in anticipation of its coming. That is now my goal in business.

When I leave for work in the morning, my prayer and my hope is that I will be prepared to drink the rain. It is a conscious effort, a mindset, a desire to look out for, and receive, the drops of wisdom and discernment that God often sends. Preparation of the ground is deliberate. It requires first that we ask, and second that we recognize. Rather than praying that God will bless your business, pray that He will send showers of wisdom and discernment and that you will be prepared to recognize and absorb them. Neither wisdom nor discernment are earthly treasures, and both are promised to us in Scripture if we earnestly and sincerely seek them.

As we apply our labor and drink the rain, we must understand the purpose greater than our own spiritual development and maturity. Hebrews 6:7 states that it brings forth "vegetation." Harvest time for the farmer is literal vegetation. I have spent many youthful hours picking vegetables and filling grain silos. Today my vegetation is no longer literal. Now my harvest is sales, growth, and profitability, but like the vegetation in the Scripture from Hebrews, my harvest has a biblical purpose. It is "useful to those for whose sake it is also tilled." This is huge, perhaps life-changing for some.

Based upon Hebrews 6:7, you and I are not in business just for ourselves. At least, we are not supposed to be. Our labor, our effort, our toil, and our risk all have a greater purpose than our personal gain.

The vegetation that has been brought forth as a joint effort between you and God is expected to benefit others. In fact, God intends it to be useful to others. He has made it clear that for their sake, the ground was tilled. A godly businessperson understands this biblical truth.

In my struggle to gain understanding into God's perspective upon the great amount of time and energy we apply to business, I have reached a conclusion. My efforts, when they are not selfishly applied, have a spiritual significance, and they become biblically relevant in a divinely orchestrated, unique form of unselfishness. It is not a willy-nilly, spread-what-we-see-fit proposition. God does not desire to use our business, or any other Christian business, to randomly commit good deeds. He intends for specific individuals and organizations out there to till the ground. What greater purpose could we achieve in business than to fulfill God's expectation in this scriptural truth?

My prayer is that the labor I do and the time I spend will become useful to *"those for whose sake it is also tilled."* The focus cannot just be upon the company's gain. We must consciously and continually seek ways that the intended others may benefit.

> *Do not withhold good from those to whom it is due,*
> *When it is in your power to do it.*
> **PROVERBS 3:27**

There is a measure of authority and power that accompanies the position of manager or owner. It "is in your power" to do good. The fallacy is that we tend to think of "good" as having to be financial. Certainly, monetary gifts are one form of doing good, but there are many more. So much potential for doing good, other than monetary, exists when you hold a position of authority. Words of praise, recognition, and appreciation from the heart and mouth of someone in a supervisory or respected role can have a special significance.

> *And how delightful is a timely word!*
> **PROVERBS 15:23**

Developing a genuine interest in the lives of those who work under your supervision communicates that they matter to you. There is no greater good than a genuine care and concern.

When we read the instruction, "Do not withhold good," we most often interpret it as a deliberate act, but another form of withholding good is an act of omission, the thing not said, the encouragement not expressed—the lack of concern over those who labor in your field. Business owners or managers who have the mindset that their employees are due nothing more than their wage are guilty of withholding good. They have ignored "those for whose sake it is also tilled." For me to try and define exactly who your vegetation was intended to be useful to would be pointless and contrary. That is something you and God need to work out together. I am still busy trying to discern my own. There are, however, three basic parameters that I believe apply to all of us.

First, I am confident that the ground is to be tilled for my household. My family is my first responsibility when I place my hand upon the plow. I must not neglect to satisfy this primary obligation. Nearly every analogy God used in Scripture describing love, devotion, and commitment was based upon family. Husband and wife are compared to Christ and His church. God the Father, Jesus the Son, and the household of faith are all examples of God's overall perspective on family.

> *He who troubles his own house will inherit wind.*
> **PROVERBS 11:29**

> *But if anyone does not provide for his own, and especially for those of his household, he has denied the faith and is worse than an unbeliever.*
> **1 TIMOTHY 5:8**

Second, the ground is to be tilled for those who labor in our field. The people who work side by side with us are due more than their wage. They are deserving of appreciation, gratitude, and a genuine concern. Those who labor beside us with integrity are due our respect, regardless of position.

What I have discovered is that this practice begins with a conscious effort. After a time, it turns into a natural extension of your business behavior. I still have much room for improvement in the application of this principle, but I see the impact that it can have. Too often, managers and owners limit communication to instructions, expectations, and the need to improve. That behavior is in no way consistent with the golden rule. On those occasions when I have the opportunity to hand out payroll checks, I shake the person's hand and thank them. The first few times I did it, I got some astonished looks. Most people have been conditioned by business to respond completely opposite. The employee should thank the employer for their wage, right? They were not sure how to take it. The principle is simple. The employee's wage is compensation for their time and ability, but I recognize that our business has benefited from their labor. If it has not, then I have managed poorly. Their effort is worthy of my appreciation beyond their financial compensation. To be regarded as valuable is gratifying and motivating, regardless of the position you hold.

The first two, family and fellow laborers, are the minimum. However, God delights when we choose to do something greater than the minimum. Career and business also have a reach, and therefore an opportunity, outside the realm of profitable commerce. The tilled ground and the rain that falls upon it produce vegetation intended by God to also benefit others who are not connected to the business. A godly businessperson desires to find ways to responsibly do good outside of the walls of business.

I want to put special emphasis on the word *responsibly*. This is the third basic parameter for doing good. Every social expectation, every need is not intended by God to be met by you. Neither is every need supposed to be ignored by you. The Scripture clearly states "those to whom it is due."

So, how are you supposed to know who is due? Again, there is nothing willy-nilly here. Drink the rain. The wisdom that falls upon us prepares us to discern when and how we should react. The communication is intimate between you and God. That is the reason it would be pointless and contrary to Scripture for me to try and define exactly what someone else should be doing with their vegetation. Seek wisdom, seek discernment, and seek knowledge. That is the purpose of intimate communication. The instruction you will receive has much more to do with motive than emotion.

I have a good friend who is an excellent, well-educated, highly regarded counselor. He was the director of a Christian ministry that deals with almost every imaginable physical, emotional, spiritual, and financial need on a daily basis. If you were to ask him what he thought presented the greatest obstacle to the services they provide, he would tell you, "The drive-bys." "Drive-bys" are those who want to toss a small bag of money or a short burst of energy at someone else's need rather than to become personally involved. It helps them to feel good about themselves because they have done something, but the root problem has been ignored and a cycle of dependency is created. The difference is simple; his burden is for the person with the need while the drive-bys feel guilty over the fact that a need exists.

For much of my business life, I have subscribed to the drive-by method of doing good. It is a one-and-done, clean-hands approach to giving back. I found ways to feel good about myself. My motive was selfish and dressed up to look concerned and charitable. My attempts not to "withhold good from those to whom it is due" were based solely upon my own definition of what was good and my own determination of to whom it was due. It had nothing to do with wisdom, discernment, or God. If what I do for a living was intended by God to be a benefit to specific individuals, I have not fulfilled His desire when I randomly choose to disperse it. Just as I pray daily for God to provide me with the wisdom and insight to conduct myself in a manner pleasing to Him, I also pray that He will allow me to understand precisely what He would like done with the vegetation.

If I endeavor to make Hebrews 6:7 the goal of my business life, and I construct my behavior within the framework of these three parameters, then there is a promise that awaits me.

> *For ground that drinks the rain which often falls on it*
> *and brings forth vegetation useful to those for whose*
> *sake it is also tilled, receives a blessing from God;*
> **HEBREWS 6:7**

Scripture says that there is a blessing from God. Based upon this verse, the blessing is for the ground that drank the rain, and I said that the ground represents your business. Therefore, the blessing is directed toward business, but that does not seem to be consistent with the assertion that God does not care about business.

Why would He promise to bless something that He does not care about?

It is an excellent question. Do not fall into the common business trap. Don't take it upon yourself to define *blessing* strictly in terms of earthly treasure. You must reconcile this verse with God's disinterest in, and warnings regarding, earthly treasure.

Businesses that are obedient to the instruction from Hebrews 6:7 are the beneficiary of blessings, as defined by God, not humans. God may certainly include financial blessings, but they are not guaranteed, and they are never alone. Nor are financial blessings supposed to be the most desired. What are some of the blessings as defined by God rather than man?

Psalm 128 outlines those things that are God's blessings. Although this passage is directed at family and community, it is also applicable to business.

> *How blessed is everyone who fears the Lord,*
> *Who walks in His ways.*
> *When you shall eat of the fruit of your hands,*
> *You will be happy and it will be well with you.*
> *Your wife shall be like a fruitful vine*
> *Within your house,*
> *Your children like olive plants*
> *Around your table.*
> *Behold, for thus shall the man be blessed*
> *Who fears the Lord.*
> *The Lord bless you from Zion,*

And may you see the prosperity of Jerusalem
all the days of your life.
Indeed, may you see your children's children.
Peace be upon Israel!

PSALM 128:1–6

God's blessings include contentment and fulfillment in our labor. We also see that He blesses men with meaningful relationships and alliances. We are able to enjoy the successes and prosperity of those we care about. He secures our future and envelops us with peace. When we understand what God considers to be blessings, we should not be surprised that He would not hesitate to use them to reward the ground that drinks the rain. The list is enticing. Wouldn't it be a shame to set our focus on earthly treasure while missing out on something with eternal value?

CHAPTER 14

GOING HOME

My quest is over. I am satisfied. I leave for work each day determined to labor diligently with biblical integrity applying all my God-given gifts: life, health, reason, insight, wisdom, and discernment. I am determined to drink the rain and not withhold good from those to whom it is due. As business owners and managers, if we are willing to do these things, then I know our labor has divine purpose. The hours spent and the energy expended have meaning. Our business hours have spiritual significance, and they yield eternal treasure that God delights in. Our single short trip across this planet has relevance and purpose beyond the accumulation of earthly treasure.

I do not claim, or even pretend, to have reached the point of consistency in this attitude and behavior. Failure lurks behind every problem, unpleasant encounter, or disappointment. Some days my soul echoes the apostle Paul's anguished confession in his letter to the church in Rome.

> *For that which I am doing, I do not understand;*
> *for I am not practicing what I would like to*
> *do, but I am doing the very thing I hate.*
>
> **ROMANS 7:15**

On those days, I console myself with the reminder from the epistle of James.

> *Consider it all joy, my brethren, when you encounter various trials, knowing that the testing of your faith produces endurance. And let endurance have its perfect result, so that you may be perfect and complete, lacking in nothing.*
>
> **JAMES 1:2–4**

The trials, the challenges, the obstacles, and the testing of faith do not end in life or in business. My moments of failure should not cause me to abandon my business mission, but rather inspire me to persevere.

Several years ago, Hal Ketchum recorded a country song, written by Tony Arata, entitled "Satisfied Mind." That song contains some of my all-time favorite lyrics. In the same way the book of Psalms contrasts the difference between foolishness and wisdom, Tony draws the contrast between true riches and monetary wealth. It is an end-of-life assessment that focuses upon living a life that pursues greater virtues and contentment. It is not God's plan, nor should it be our desire, to live this life forever. The song ends with a powerful testimony, about not wanting more than was his and returning home satisfied.

Returning to the bigger barns parable, having filled his barns to overflowing was not the tragic mistake the rich man made. As discussed earlier, full barns can be the product of hard work, obedience, and godly wisdom. Solomon had full barns. Losing his life that very night was not even the great tragedy for the rich landowner. Nor was it the great tragedy for my fictitious character, Robert, in the preface. Death was inevitable for both of these men at some point. Unless the Lord returns first, death awaits us all.

> *And inasmuch as it is appointed for men to die…*
> **HEBREWS 9:27**

Though inescapable, based upon Scripture, death is the pathway to our eternal existence. In the case of Robert at least, to be absent from the body is to be present with the Lord. The condition is described in 2 Corinthians 5:8. In fact, the death of a believer is precious to the Lord.

> *Precious in the sight of the Lord*
> *Is the death of His godly ones.*
> **PSALM 116:15**

The tragedy for both men was that they could not go home with a satisfied mind. Neither will you or I if we cling to the notion that earthly treasure has spiritual relevance. We will stare at the place our bigger barns would have stood, brokenhearted over what we traded for them. Business will seem irrelevant in contrast to God's stars glimmering in the velvet black sky. You will pass from the earth with business contracts won and eternal opportunities lost. In an instant you will see business from the Lord's perspective. Your business is nothing more than a tool. It is a hammer in the hand of a carpenter, a plow in the hands of a farmer.

God has no desire or interest in blessing the hammer or the plow. Don't ask Him to do so. Ask Him to bless the hand and the heart. Ask Him to send the things that you are unable to manufacture. "*Send the rain, Lord, and allow me to understand for whose sake the ground is also tilled.*" If in the process the barns become full, then you have applied skill and diligence to the tools in your hand. Just know that the full barn is not how God will measure your success. God does not care about business, and in the end neither will you. All that will matter someday is to lie down and go home with a satisfied mind. Hallelujah.

ABOUT THE AUTHOR

Richard J. Grove is a mechanical designer, inventor, and entrepreneur. The products he has developed and patented form the backbone of what has grown into a multi-million dollar family-owned and operated business.

Richard has been a student of the Bible and a Bible study teacher for over 30 years. He resides just east of Atlanta, Georgia with his wife, Lisa. They have three adult children who are actively involved in the business. They have also been blessed with four wonderful grandchildren.

www.ingramcontent.com/pod-product-compliance
Lightning Source LLC
LaVergne TN
LVHW041334080426
835512LV00006B/448